A Country Life

A Country Life

by William S. Morse

Moose Country Press
1995

Moose Country Press
Warren, N.H.

ISBN 0-9642213-1-4

Library of Congress Cataloging-in-Publication Data

Morse, William S. (William Sanders) , 1904–
    A country life / by William S. Morse.
        p.   cm.
    ISBN 0-9642213-1-4 (pbk.)
    1. Country life -- New England -- History --
20th century. 2. New England -- Social life and customs.
3. Morse, William S. (William Sanders) ,1904– --
Childhood and youth.   I. Title.
F9.M67   1994
974'.04'092 — dc20
[B]   94-43017
                                                  CIP

10 9 8 7 6 5 4 3 2 1

For my grandchildren,
Dee and Erin,
and my great grandchildren,
Shelby and Ashley,
and for those who come after.

There was a time, when I was a boy, when life was much different than the one you are experiencing.

We did not have autos or movies or radio or television. The air age was years in the future. The electronic age and space age were even further away. Life was much simpler and uncluttered — we were more concerned with the basics of living. There was a rural America then not much different from that of our ancestors.

I thought that you might like to know something of our way of life, and I have tried to portray it as I remember it.

Contents

Introduction by Noel Perrin

Introduction

If a rural New Englander lives long enough --
I'd say 75 is the minimum acceptable, and 80 or
90 is better -- he or she gets to be an old-timer. At
least within their own towns, old-timers enjoy a
number of privileges. They can speak out of turn
at town meeting, provided they don't do it too
often. They can freely practice the kind of put-
down that in a younger person would be called
rudeness. With them it's called being tart. (I'm
not saying that all old-timers <u>are</u> tart; some
wouldn't dream of putting down even the
brashest young city slicker. I'm just saying they're
licensed to be.)

But the chief prerogative of old-timers, of
course, is that they get to talk about the old times,
while other people eagerly listen.

About the old times themselves, old-timers are seldom tart. On the contrary, they usually inject a golden haze into the air. Those were the days! The days when everybody knew everybody else in town, and not only knew them but recognized their sleigh bells. You'd hear jingles on a moonlit December night, and you'd say," There goes young Albert Johnson -- he must be plannin' to call on the Fifield girls. And that's old Earl Boisvert comin' the other way. Lettin' the hoss drive as usual." What a contrast to the anonymous roar of the automobile traffic going by now.

Bill Morse is a different kind of old-timer. He meets every qualification: turned 90 this year, grew up on a farm, enjoys reminiscing about the past. But there is little or no golden haze. Get him talking about what fun it was to ride in a one-horse open sleigh, and yes, indeed, he'll remember the pleasure. It was real. He'll also remind you that in the sleigh "the only thing between you and the rear end of a horse is a low dashboard that does not offer much of a barrier to the discharges of a horse, especially when he is in a gaseous condition. " And he'll remember that sometimes you got so cold in a sleigh, even if you had buffalo robes and bearskins, that you'd get out and run alongside for a half a mile, hoping to warm up a little. Very sensible. But not very Currier and Ivesish.

Morse looks back in an equally clear-eyed way on old-fashioned sugaring (it was exhausting work, lugging those sap pails) and haying. (No city person has any idea how fantastically hot it gets in a hayloft in July.) Then there's the role the cow's tail plays in hand-milking, and so on right round the farm and the village. Since Bill Morse is good at evoking scenes, the result is a fascinating account of old-time New England the way it really was. Put another way, the result is this book.

Noel Perrin

A Country Life

Bill Morse
Mt. Moosilauke, 1915

The Country Life

Today's generations are quite far removed in years from the days in which old Dobbin held sway. Their impressions of life as it was lived in the distant past are formed from pictures of the Currier and Ives sort, some of which show horses gaily pulling sleighs across a winter landscape. Many of the pictures depict well-maintained farmhouses which have plumes of woodsmoke rising from their chimneys. They all conjure up an image of a delightful rural life – an image which has often been

romanticized and enhanced by nostalgia. There are
some who express a desire to return to those times.
If they did, they would soon find out that such images
are illusions.

Our most factual images of life as it was lived
in the distant past are best obtained from first-hand
accounts of those who experienced it. My life's span
extends back into the first decade of this century and
includes the final years of what has generally become
known as the horse and buggy days. Although it takes
some temerity to do so, I shall attempt to describe what
rural life was like as I remember experiencing it in a
spot of New England in those years. It was not as
delightful as many like to portray it.

There is an area in the west central part of New
Hampshire known simply as Number Six, which
encompasses the foot hills of the Hog Back range of
mountains. It was there that my ancestors settled, and
it was there that I was born soon after the turn of the
century. Home delivery was the custom in those days,
and I was born in the same house in which my father
was born.

My father often told me tales of our ancestors
and stories of his experiences that described what life
was like in his younger days. I have a good remem-
brance of my childhood and boyhood years in the first
two decades of this century, which were spent growing
up in a strictly rural environment of hillside farms:
an environment that sometimes seems light years
away from the world of today.

Our life was not as harsh as that of my father's
early days. One of the episodes that he related to me
was of an experience he had with a terrific toothache

when he was ten years old. His tooth became so painful that his parents decided it would have to be pulled. There were no dentists around in those days, and doctors were very scarce. If a doctor was not readily available people often resorted to a blacksmith who was experienced in pulling horses' teeth. In my father's case the blacksmith was the nearest. My grandfather gave him a silver dollar and saddled a horse that my father rode over the hills for a distance of several miles to the blacksmith, whose name was Glazier. Glazier made him take a drink of rum, set him on an upended block of wood, clamped some horse forceps on his tooth and pulled it out, after which he had him take another slug of rum. I asked if it hurt badly, and my father said that it hurt like hell, but he felt that the ordeal of drinking the rum was worse than pulling the tooth. He was at a tender age to make the acquaintance of hard liquor, and he said that Glazier's rum was so strong and thick and raw that it could almost be cut with a knife.

That incident occurred in the early eighteen eighties. By the time I came around, about twenty years later, the dental profession had made its appearance, and laughing gas had replaced rum as the means of easing the pain of pulling a tooth. A few other similar changes had taken place, but in general the style and manner of life in our area and the surrounding countryside was not very much different from that of my father's early years.

We traveled the same rough dirt roads, transported by horses pulling buggies and wagons in the summer and sleighs and bob sleds in the winter. We went to the same one-room school that our parents had attended before us, where the three R's were pounded into our heads by stern and frustrated teachers. Most of us lived in the old weatherbeaten houses that our ancestors had built, and which had changed very little over the years. The chills and blasts of winter were lessened by stoves that had to be constantly fed with wood which had been laboriously cut and prepared with axe and bucksaw the previous winter. It took a lot of wood to keep those old houses warm and to supply the cook stove throughout the year – at least twelve or fifteen cords. One of the ways in which a man was judged in those days was by the size and quality of his woodpile.

As a rule only one room besides the kitchen had a stove. A large cooking range took care of the kitchen, and a tall Round Oak stove kept the adjoining room, which was called the sitting room, warm. The other rooms of the house were closed off and were unheated. They seemed to absorb and store up all of the cold that a northern New England winter could produce. That was especially true of the bedrooms. When you arose to start the day and your bare feet hit the cold floor on a ten or twenty below morning you didn't waste any time getting into some clothes and rushing downstairs to the warmth of the kitchen.

When you answered the calls of nature you went out to an isolated privy where you sat on a crudely carved hole while your nether ends were caressed by hordes of flies in the summer and by icy blasts of air in the winter. In either case you made sure you had to go before you went, and you could fully expect that the place would be vacant. People did not dawdle long in such an environment. Sanitary needs were taken care of by old newspapers and catalogues, and there was usually a string of corncobs hanging on a nail. My grandfather, who often lived with us, used mullein leaves. He claimed that they helped his piles.

When you took a bath you were given the privacy of the kitchen where you soaked and scrubbed yourself while sitting in a metal tub that was placed in front of the stove. The Saturday night bath was a tradition in our house, and my mother was very insistent that everyone observe it. It was the custom in those days for the hired man to live with us, and he was considered as part of the family. We had one who quit his job because, as he put it, he didn't "cotton to taking a bath every week." He had plenty of company. I am certain that there were people who went all winter without taking a bath.

People went to the barn by the dim light of the early dawn where they fed and hand milked a herd of cows by lantern light before breakfast. The barns were not like the cozy cow parlors of today. Often they were not much more than a shelter, and they were cold in the winter. There was hardly any mechanization. The gasoline age was in its diapers and would not begin to make itself felt for well over another decade. Manpower and horsepower were the moving forces in those early years of the century. Life was quite toilsome, and living was somewhat Spartan.

The village, which served as the hub of our universe, was alongside the railroad down in the river valley. It was small, and offered but little in the way of facilities. Besides the railroad station, known as the Depot, there was a small country store that also contained the post office. A creamery, which received the milk produced by the farms of the surrounding countryside, employed a few people. A saw mill that was in an adjoining pasture was quite busy and furnished employment for a number of residents. The only person who could be called an artisan was the blacksmith who kept the area's horses shod and its buggies rolling. The professional roster was filled by the ever-present horse trader, and there was a livestock dealer who collected canners and other poor specimens that he shipped to the abattoir at Brighton for city consumption. We used to watch them being loaded into cattle cars and feel sorry for the poor souls who had to eat them. Social amenities were provided by the Grange. Its hall served as the community center, and a small church provided the area with its needs for salvation. A widow, who lived at the east end of the village and provided food for gossip, should probably be added to complete the list of establishments.

The adjoining village, five miles to the west, was devoted to manufacturing. It had the distinction of supplying the world with its whetstones and scythestones, and its factory and quarries were busy. Otherwise, however, it was just another rural village that did not even offer the diversity that our small hamlet enjoyed. Its main attraction was the company store, which was really a rural department store with a barber shop and a pool table. A trip to it from our foot hills was the equivalent of a trip to the metropolis. The journey, behind the plodding of Old Dobbin, spoiled the better part of a day and was an excursion.

The style of living followed by the residents of the villages did not differ greatly from those who lived on the farms. Their homes were heated by stoves and wood, and the privy was the throne of the day. The company store may have had a hopper instead of a privy, but I cannot remember one. Local travel in the first decades was mostly by horse and buggy. If a family had a horse they had to have a small barn to keep it in and a small field to furnish it with fodder. A few people might have a cow, and some kept a few chickens. The farmer on a hillside farm made more extensive use of the land and felt that he enjoyed more independence; otherwise there was not much difference in their manner of living. Each residence had its plot of land that could serve as a small farm. Today it would be called subsistence living, but I cannot recall ever hearing that term used. Present day bureaucrats would probably be quick to point out that such a manner of living is perilously close to what they call the poverty level, but no one gave any thought to such a thing in those days. It was the rural way of life at that time, and people were thankful for what they had.

Dobbin

Unless one was going far enough away from his home grounds to use the railroad, travel in the horse and buggy days was a very slow and time-consuming process. It would be difficult for the present generation to imagine what travel was like when there were no paved roads; when all of the roads were dirt, and the only travel over them was by foot or by horse drawn vehicles. The distance that can be traveled today in a little over half an hour would require a full day of travel behind old Dobbin; travel that could be tedious and unpleasant in any season of the year.

In the spring there were stretches of road that were rivers of mud in which wagon wheels would sink to their hubs and axles. Often a person would have to get out of whatever he was riding in, and wallow knee deep in the mud to help horse his vehicle through it. Some spots could get so bad that the horses themselves would get mired and have to be pulled out. Many such places had been filled in over the years with brush and logs that eventually hit bottom, creating a corduroy road so rough and washboardy that it could loosen your teeth when you rode over it.

When the mud dried up in the summer, it became dirt and dust that would rise around you in clouds when stirred up by the horse's hooves. When you arrived anywhere at the end of a trip, your clothes would be covered with a liberal amount of dirt and dust and horsehair, and often a bit of excrement besides. In case you have never ridden in a buggy, it should be pointed out that the only thing between you and the rear end of a horse is a low dashboard that does not offer much of a barrier to the discharges of a horse, especially when he is in a gaseous condition. Often, when a horse was off his feed, he would be fed some molasses mixed with his oats which served to stir up his insides enough so that he was explosive, and it could be hazardous to ride behind him. If the molasses happened to be sulphured the atmosphere could become decidedly smelly. When you took a girl friend to some social event, things could sometimes get embarrassing.

I have read articles that extolled the joys and delights of the horse and buggy. I think that depiction is a myth which should be exploded. In our area in those days people did not ride for pleasure. They rode to get somewhere or to transport something. If one had a simple errand a mile or so away, he didn't bother to harness a horse and hitch him to a buggy. He walked.

Snow drifts and cold were the nemesis of winter travel when everything was on runners. There were numerous types of winter conveyances. Sleighs were used for light and fast travel. Many were quite fancy. Some had high sides and dashboards, and one sat deep inside them. A few were colorful and brightly decorated, with combinations of red, black, and yellow predominating. Bobsleds, that were large heavy sleds coupled in tandem, were used for heavy loads and rough travel. For some reason, whenever they were painted, their color was blue. One-horse pungs were the most popular rigs. A pung was a light wagon box with a seat that was mounted on sleigh runners. It was light and fast and could carry quite a load.

All of the conveyances were open air vehicles which left a person exposed to the wind and the cold. For warmth and protection people had to wear heavy clothes, and they wrapped themselves in buffalo and bearskin robes. If it was real cold, it was not unusual for one to run alongside his rig to keep from freezing. If one encountered a sleet storm or a blizzard, he and old Dobbin were in for a harsh time. A wind-blown snow drift could block all progress. If you tried to negotiate your way around it you stood a good chance of tipping over and rolling in the snow. The only alternative was to shovel a way through it. The jolly jingle of sleigh bells did not suffice to make winter travel a pleasure.

One of the earliest remembrances of my childhood is of a trip that I took with my mother on a cold winter day. We went to the county seat in

William S. Morse

Woodsville, a distance of twelve or more miles, in a sleigh with a high dashboard. We had some soapstones with us that had spent the previous night getting hot in the oven of the kitchen stove. They were placed on the floor of the sleigh, and by wrapping our legs in heavy robes we kept warm by trapping the heat as it rose from the stones. We left home early in the morning, and arrived back in the evening, guided by the light of a lantern hung on the dashboard.

The roads were not plowed in the winter. They were rolled and packed by snow rollers, which were much more exciting than any snowplow could possibly be. A big snow roller was an imposing thing. It had two large rollers made of wood, and each had slatted wooden treads. The large heavy duty rollers were six feet or so in diameter, and they were hollow. A person could walk through them. They were set side by side so that the two of them spanned the entire width of the road, and the frame in which they were housed was constructed in a way that allowed it to be loaded with stones to provide whatever weight was necessary to pack the snow. The driver was perched on a seat on top of the frame eight feet or more in the air. He had to be a capable horseman, for there were never less than four horses hitched to the roller, and often there were six or eight horses pulling it. The driver was usually aware of his importance. His horses were well groomed. Their harnesses were oiled and polished and festooned with sleigh bells. The huge roller with the long string of horses pulling it was an impressive sight.

The crunch of the rollers packing the cold snow, and the jingle of the sleigh bells would herald the approach of the roller when it was a half-mile away, and every kid who was able to duck his chores would grab his sled and head for the hills. The newly packed snow offered the fastest and best sliding which could be found. That is one bit of fun we had that cannot be enjoyed by the kids today. We got our thrills by belly bumping on a sled down the longest, steepest and crookedest hills that we could find, often going a mile or more, and then trudging back to do it all over again. Everyone was able to join in the fun, for no expense was involved. Our sleds were hand made. The well packed roads were free and made to order, and were practically in our own back yards. The competition to see whose sled was the fastest and which would coast the greatest distance was fierce.

The arrival of the snowroller was not a frequent occurrence. It only came around after a heavy snowstorm. It was not a tax and spend era in those days. A farmer was expected to keep his stretch of road passable until the elements overwhelmed him, and he managed to do so by shoveling and dragging it with a bob sled. He was happy to make any contribution that would keep taxes down. Until a storm was heavy enough to bring out the rollers the roads were kept passable, but there were always plenty of snow drifts and rough spots for a man and his horse to contend with.

Webster defines a Dobbin as a slow, plodding, farm or family horse, and that is what most of them were. A countryman and his horse shared the tedious drudgery of toil and travel in all seasons of the year and in every sort of weather. They became quite dependent upon each other. A man took care of his horse, and there could be times when his horse took care of him. Cider flowed freely in those days. There were some who had a propensity for it, and there were times when a man might find himself some distance from home and unable to function properly. All that he had to do in such a case was to make it to his sleigh or buggy and Dobbin would take care of the task of getting him safely home. The horse knew the way; he did not need any guidance, and he knew what was expected of him. As a result of sharing their many vicissitudes a great affinity often developed between a man and his horse. There is the story of a farmer's lament upon the death of his wife. "God," he said, "I'd rather lost my horse."

During the first decade of the century automobiles were in their first stages of production. They were starting to make their appearance in the cities, which were far from our area, and they were seldom encountered on our rural roads. Our poor roads were no enticement to them, and in our neck of the woods they were a curiosity and more or less of a nuisance until well into the second decade. The chances of their replacing old Dobbin seemed remote.

Most of the rural areas had one other means of travel that, along with the horse and buggy, has been erased from the scene in many places. The railroad connecting Boston and Montreal ran through our valley. It served the hamlets along its way by hauling their products the long distance to the cities and their markets. It also carried passengers. My grandfather claimed that the railroads were the cause of our poor country roads. Before the railroads came, teams and stagecoaches transported produce and people the long distance to the cities, and they needed and had, for those days, good roads. The railroads changed all of that by taking the place of the teams and the coaches, making their long haul unnecessary. As a result the roads became neglected and went to pot. My grandfather may have had a point. There is quite a bit of irony in the fact that many of the old stage roads are just a path in the woods, and now a large number of the old railroad beds with their tracks torn up are rapidly approaching the same condition.

In those early century years people traveled on the railroad if they were going a long distance, but the rural nature of our countryside made it impractical for local trips of ten or fifteen miles or so. Within that radius of distance people depended upon old Dobbin to haul them around.

The long freight trains, and especially the huge steam locomotives, were exciting, and along with the horse and buggy have become the object of much nostalgia. Today an old steam locomotive is a curiosity and a tourist trap. The long, lonesome, loonlike wail of its whistle echoing through the valleys is a thing of the distant past, along with the slow, patient plodding of old Dobbin.

William S. Morse

Chores

A kid growing up on a family hillside farm in the early years of the century soon learned that chores were plentiful and that he was supposed to handle his share of them. The early ones that were assigned to him were quite easy. They were sort of enjoyable at first, but as one grew older his chores kept pace by growing with him. No matter how trivial they seemed, one quickly learned that they were important, that people depended upon their being done, and that they were one's responsibility. A kid was taken to task if he was not prompt and diligent in doing them.

The first chore that I remember becoming involved with was that of keeping the kitchen wood

box filled. A kitchen range had a small fire box, and
the wood for it was finely split and of small size.
When a kid was around five years old he could handle
a few sticks of it, and that was when his working career
began. Our kitchen wood box was a large one that was
set against the wall on the reservoir side of the stove.
A partition divided it into two bins. One bin was for
wood that would make a quick hot fire, such as birch,
ash, and softwoods. The other bin was for wood that
would burn hot and slow such as maple, beech, and
oak, which my mother used for baking. A fellow
learned about the different species of wood at an early
age.

When one became able to handle big and heavy
chunks of wood, the chore of supplying the large stove
in the sitting room was added to his duties. Keeping
wood boxes filled sounds like a trivial matter, but
it was not as simple as it appears. It was quite an
important task as all of the cooking in those days was
done by a wood fire. In our house I had some help
from the rest of the household. Our privy was at the
far end of the woodshed. After visiting it, almost
everyone would grab some wood to carry in to the
main house. An epidemic of the trots could ease a
kid's wood toting burden.

Another chore which was always around in
those days was that of turning a crank. If those of
today's generation could be transported back to the
early years of the century they would quickly realize
what a boon electricity is. Before it arrived – and it was
awfully slow in getting to the rural areas – almost
everything on a farm was made to operate by turning
a crank.

William S. Morse

My mother's washing apparatus could hardly be called a machine by any stretch of the imagination. It was a rather long, narrow bench with a clothes wringer attached across the center of it. A wash tub with a scrub board was on one side of the wringer, and a tub of rinse water was on the other side. After the clothes were scrubbed and washed, they were transferred to the rinse tub by cranking them through the rollers of the wringer. After they were rinsed, they had to be cranked through the wringer again before they were hung out to dry. It could be hard cranking when sheets and heavy clothes were being washed. Cranking clothes through the wringer was supposed to be a girl's chore, but as I didn't have any sisters, my mother relied on me for the job.

The process of making butter required a double dose of cranking. Many of the farms in our area made their own butter and took any surplus which they had to the store for credit. In order to obtain the cream, whole milk had to be cranked through rapidly turning discs of a separator, which separated the cream from the milk. The machine had two spouts on it. Cream came out of one spout and skimmed milk came out of the other. The cream then had to be made into butter by placing it in a churn and cranking the thing until the butter came. Butter seemed to be temperamental. Sometimes it would come quickly, and at other times one would have to crank for half an hour before it came. I do not believe that oleo was in existence in those days. I remember when it first came on the market in our area. It was awful stuff. It was white and looked like lard. People derided it.

Another cranking chore occurred in the fall

when we butchered to obtain our winter's meat. My mother made a lot of sausage and mincemeat, and the meat was ground up by cranking chunks of it through a large meat grinder. Beef critters and pigs do not grind up very easily. The grinder was a large one that took big chunks of meat, and it was hard work cranking it. The crank handle was big enough so that one could get both hands on it. They were needed.

One cranking chore that a fellow did not object to was cranking the ice cream freezer. The treat that resulted was ample recompense for the cranking. It was real ice cream, made only of cream and eggs with nothing ersatz in it.

There were a few other things around the house that operated by turning a crank, but they were a picnic compared to what one ran into outside. Turning a grindstone was probably the hardest cranking chore. Many things on a farm needed sharpening – axes, scythes, section bar knives from the mowing machine and all sorts of tools. The grindstones were large, about twenty-four inches in diameter. They were thick and heavy and had to be turned rapidly. The person doing the grinding put a lot of pressure on the stone – often enough to almost stop it from turning – and he was continually yelling for it to be cranked harder and faster. It took both hands on the crank handle and all the strength that one could muster. Often that was not enough.

Another gut buster that had to be cranked was the corn sheller. We had a one holer. You shoved an ear of corn in the hole and cranked it through some ragged rollers which ripped the kernels off the cob. The kernels fell into a bucket and were fed to the hens.

William S. Morse

The cobs came out with a clean shave and were dried and used to smoke hams. Not much was wasted in those days.

A close runner-up to turning a crank was pushing a pump handle. Unless a farm was fortunate enough to have a hillside spring that could be piped to the buildings, it had to get its water from a dug well. I guess our well was about fifteen feet deep. I suppose our ancestors obtained their water from it by bailing it out with a bucket. We had progressed to a hand pump. Pumping water wasn't a bad chore in the summer when the cows were out to pasture where they could get all the water they needed. It was a different story in the winter. The cows were watered twice a day. A pail of water is just a teaser to a cow, and a herd of fifteen or twenty of them needs a lot of water. It had to be pumped whether the weather was balmy or ten or twenty below zero. "Cold as a pump handle in January" is an old Yankee saying which describes the ordeal.

Water was a big problem on many of the farms in those days. A dowser found water on the hill above us, and we stoned up a large reservoir from which we piped water to the buildings. That was a red letter event, but the reservoir always went dry in the coldest part of the winter, and we would have to return to pushing the old pump handle.

A chore involving some responsibility that was handed to a kid at an early age was taking care of the hens. I became acquainted with chickens long before I was given the chore of taking care of them. We used to buy our chicks in the spring from a mail order house. They would arrive when they were only a few days old. My mother would make a small pen behind the kitchen stove, put some papers on the floor, and turn the chicks loose in the pen. She would keep them there until they were acclimated and large enough to get out of the pen and start roaming around the kitchen. Fifty chicks chirping and roaming around the room had to be fascinating things to a one or two year old child.

We kept about fifty hens which were enough to keep us in eggs and furnish us with an occasional meal. They had the run of the farmyard in the summer, and kept the bugs and table scraps cleaned up. The chore of taking care of them in the warmer months was easy. All one had to do was throw them a little corn and gather the eggs. Their care in the winter was more demanding. They had to be fed warm mash, their water containers had to be kept free of ice, and they had to have plenty of straw and bedding on the floor. One also had to keep a sharp eye out for foxes and weasels that were constantly trying to get into the hen house where they would cause havoc if they succeeded. I used to set traps for them, and usually caught several during a winter. A prime red fox fur was worth a fair piece of change in those days.

There were a great variety of breeds of hens many of which I imagine have been hybridized out of existence today. Over the years we had Rhode Island Reds, Plymouth Rocks, White Leghorns, Black Minorcas, Purple Andalusians, and many others, the names of which I have forgotten. When they were out running free they added quite a bit of color to the yard. We also kept a few guinea hens. We raised them for food for they are good to eat. They are very gamey, almost like a partridge. They did not mix much with the rest of the hens. At night they roosted in the orchard, which was near the house, and were as good as a watch dog. They made an ungodly racket if anyone came around at night. They were also an alarm clock. They made such a noise at sunup that they woke everyone up. Early mornings on the farm were quite noisy. The clacking of the hens, the crowing of the roosters, and the lowing of the cows anxious to be fed created a medley of sounds, announcing that a new day had started and that there was work to be done.

Keeping wood boxes filled and taking care of the hens were routine chores that had to be done daily, and the result of neglecting them was quick to show up. They required some diligence and attention. Cranking things and pushing a pump handle were intermittent chores that occurred frequently. They did not involve much intelligence or responsibility. All one had to do was to attach himself to a crank or a pump handle and start working. Our elders in those days seemed to think that such chores were too insignificant for a grown person, and whenever possible a kid was collared for the job.

Today's push button age has made such chores obsolete. Our modern conveniences are so commonplace that they are not properly appreciated by the present generation.

School

"Readin' and 'Ritin' and 'Rithmetic, taught to the tune of the hickory stick" are the words of an old song. The ditty defines the subjects that were taught in the one room school houses of the early years of the century. It also describes one of the methods used to teach them.

Those one room school houses were old. The one in our district was about one hundred years old when I began attending it in 1909. There were a lot of them of the same age scattered around the countryside, which in my time consisted almost entirely of hillside farms. In their early years of settlement the towns of northern New England were divided into numerous school districts in order to provide learning facilities for children within a walking range of one or two country miles. The districts were sparsely settled and the school houses were small, built to accommodate twelve or fifteen pupils. All of the eight grades were taught in them by one teacher. Some grades had but one or two kids.

The school house in our district was not the little red school house of song and story. It was painted white, and had been designed to segregate the sexes as much as possible. There were two entrances at the front of the building. Each one led to a small cloak room, or entry, as it was called. The entry on the right was for the girls and the one on the left was for the boys. Beyond the cloak rooms was the class room, which had an aisle down its center with desks on each side facing the rear wall of the room. Each desk and seat were joined together in one unit. They were old and beat up: ink-stained, and carved with the initials and art work of the generations who had used them before us. The girls occupied the desks on the right side of the aisle, and the boys sat at the ones on the left. A platform at the rear of the room was the teacher's domain where she had us stand to recite our lessons. Outside, tacked on to the rear end of the building, was a woodshed with two privies. To use the privies one had to go out the front door and walk around the building; an unpleasant trip in cold and stormy weather.

A large box stove stood near the cloak room wall, and it had to work hard to keep the room warm in zero weather. Taking care of the school house was a cooperative effort. The families that had children at school supplied the firewood, and the older boys took weekly turns acting as janitor, arriving early to start the fire and to sweep the floor. Almost all of the boys had barn and stable chores to do before going to school in the morning. They were not very choosy about changing their clothes, and on days when the windows had to be closed, the air in the school room was strongly suggestive of the barn and the cows and the stable.

All of the teachers who taught at our school when I attended my first eight grades were women, and we had a different teacher each year. Some of them were young, and were on their first teaching assignment. They were hotly pursued by the swains of the area. Others were older and more experienced with their discipline.

Teaching a bunch of country kids in those one room schools must have been a difficult job. The teacher had to start from scratch with the ones who were beginning the first grade. There were no preschool programs at that time. A lot of us were not very enthused about having to attend school, and some of the older boys were more intent upon finding ways to plague the teacher than they were in learning. Baiting the teacher was a pastime. Discipline was necessary, and the hickory stick or its counterpart was used quite often. When they hired a teacher the school boards were as interested in a teacher's ability to keep discipline – to "trim them out" as it was called – as they were in her ability to teach.

Most of the punishment was routine. The youngest children received a birch switch across their legs when they were unruly. A favorite weapon for punishment was a heavy two foot hardwood ruler that the teacher carried with her most of the time. A teacher with a quick eye could give you a sharp rap

across the knuckles or on the side of the head before
you knew it was coming. It hurt, and it was quite
effective when one was being playful or dense in
learning his lessons. One year we had an old tartar
who carried a rubber hose. She had a short temper,
and it didn't take much provocation for her to lay the
hose across your shoulders.

I cannot recall any objections from the parents
about the punishments that the kids received at
school. A teacher was supposed to keep discipline.
The punishment that she doled out was probably more
lenient than that which the kids received at home
when they were stubborn or unruly. It was the custom
for the teacher to room and board in the district, and
often she did so at our house. My father had a set
routine with a new teacher. He would tell her in my
presence that she was not to show any partiality
towards me because of the fact that she was staying
at our house. His exact words were: "If he needs a
trimming, you trim him!" He would then inform me
that if I came home bellyaching about receiving a
trimming at school, he would give me another one.
The old adage of spare the rod and spoil the child
was given considerable credence in those days. The
corrections that we received did not seem to do us any
harm and were probably beneficial to us. It taught us
respect for our elders and the morals of that time.

The people of the district made certain that they
were getting their money's worth from the teacher.
The mothers took turns in visiting school for half a
day or so in order to observe how the teacher was
doing. A member of the school board would often
drop in unexpectedly and fire questions at us to see if

we were learning anything. I guess a teacher had to be on her toes most of the time.

I am quite certain that attending school was mandatory then, but the regulation did not seem to be enforced. Kids started school at all ages from five years and up. It was easy to get excused from school if one was needed for work on the farm. Some kids didn't go to school. My father had a logging camp a mile or so from the school house. A family who worked for him had two boys of school age. The youngest one helped his mother who cooked for the camp, and the oldest one, who was about my age, helped his father cut and skid logs. Every time I went up to the camp with my father, I envied them.

As I recall almost all of the girls finished the eighth grade, but the boys were not as motivated. Quite a few of them dropped out without finishing school. They would drop out to go to work, either on the family farm or some other place. Jobs were plentiful at that time. There was hardly any mechanization, and the majority of the jobs involved hard manual labor, but one who grew up on a hillside farm was used to that.

I do not remember much about the books that we studied. I can recall Spot and Dick and Jane in what was probably the first book we had that associated letters with names and things. I remember very well the first real story book that we read. It was a small, well-illustrated book, titled *The Overall Boys*, which was about the activities of a family of farm boys. Our spelling book was a long narrow book with a long listing of words on its pages. It looked like a laundry list. All that I can remember of our arithmetic book is that it had a list of problems at the end of each chapter. My grandfather and I used to argue over them when I studied it at home in the evening. He was more interested in it than I was.

In spite of all of the vexations that we caused them, and in spite of the handicaps that they had to contend with, our teachers managed to drive some knowledge and learning into our heads. Those of us who made it through the eighth grade were able to read and write and we could figure. We also had a smattering of history and geography, and we were prepared to enter the high schools of that time.

For most of the kids the eighth grade was the end of the road. A distant cousin and I were the only ones in our district who continued on to high school, which was an effort in those days. The nearest high school was over ten miles and a couple of villages away, and we were on our own in finding a way to attend it. Automobiles were a novelty, and buses had yet to make their appearance. Old Dobbin still held sway for local travel, and the distance was too much for him to cope with daily.

Fortunately, we were able to commute by train. The railroad gave us a special fare. It was a hike of over a mile from our farm to the railroad station in the village, and on the other end it was a mile hike from the station to the school. The procedure had to be reversed after school was out. By the time one's evening chores were done one had put in a long day. Most of the kids were not able to cope with it or else they were not motivated enough. My motivation came from my parents.

In the first two decades of this century America

was predominantly rural. It is estimated that there were over 200,000 one room schools scattered around the country. One half of the kids attending school at that time received the basics of their education and had their characters shaped in them. They then went on to become part of the warp and woof of the fabric that gave America its prestige.

There are a few one room schools operating today, but they are evidently having a hard time coping with the regulations that are set by our present bureaucratic boards of education. A recent newspaper account tells of a one room Amish school of fifteen desks in Wisconsin which is being hassled because it is not meeting state building regulations. According to reports, there are also some one room schools in northern Vermont which are being forced to close because they fail to meet state building requirements. In both of these cases the debate appears to be over building regulations instead of the quality of education which the kids are receiving.

Today's system of mass education with its palaces of learning and the many subjects and amenities which are offered to the children are a far cry from the horse and buggy methods of those early years. Yet, there are many people who find modern schooling worrisome, and consider its results to be somewhat barren. They feel that there is something lacking, and that our future will not be as great as that of our past.

William S. Morse

Helping Out

Chores had a counterpart that was
usually known as "helping out." There was a
difference between the two. Chores involved a daily
routine or jobs that occurred frequently, whereas
helping out was something that was done momen-
tarily and might never be done again. It was something that a kid often got roped in to do when an extra
helping hand was useful or a job was distasteful.

The hired man might be oiling a harness, which
is a messy job. The harness was disassembled, and its
parts were soaked in harness oil that was rubbed and
worked into the leather, making it pliable and giving it
a longer life. If you happened to come around while
he was doing it, the hired man would be quick to

29

transfer some of the mess to you by inveigling you into helping out. The results were twofold. First, you learned how to oil a harness, which might or might not prove to be of some value in the future. Secondly, if you found the job disagreeable, you learned to make yourself scarce when you saw it being done again.

Helping out was instructive; a young fellow learned how to do many things. It was done with older people, and one gained a sense of belonging and of learning to be useful. It served to bridge the gap between the early chores that stayed with a boy during his school years, and conditioned him for those that came later, which could more properly be called work.

The summer vacation from school coincided with the haying season. A young fellow started his apprenticeship by hand-raking the scatterings with a big bull rake that was almost as large as himself, and then progressed to driving the horse rake and helping to cock the windrows of hay. My father took great pride in the neat appearance of his fields: the edges along the walls and the rough spots had to be hand trimmed with a scythe. It took me a long time to learn to swing one of those things, and I never liked the job. If one mowed into a hornets' nest there was hell to pay. As time went on and one grew larger and stronger he completed the course by pitching hay onto the hayrack, and wrestling with it while storing it in the bays and under the eaves of the barn. Today the smell of new mown hay drying in the field brings back memories of those early years, but they are not the least bit nostalgic. They are memories of toiling in the hot sun, pitching heavy forkfuls of hay seven or eight feet up in the air to someone topping off a big load of hay, and then of sweating while stowing it away under the roof of a stifling hot and airless barn.

A lot of the farm work that was seasonal is not done today. The milk that was produced had to be cooled before it was taken to the creamery, which called for a lot of ice during the summer months. Getting in the ice was a winter job in which a young fellow often participated. The ice was cut on a mill pond in the village, and it was done during the coldest part of the winter when the ice would be around eighteen inches thick. The job was not mechanized. The ice was cut into long strips with a hand pulled ice saw. Large square blocks were then cut off the strips with ice chisels, loaded onto sleds, and hauled to the farm where they were stored by burying them in sawdust in an insulated ice house. As I recall, we used to put up about seven hundred cakes of ice. All of the farms cut their ice at the same time and it often became a cooperative effort. A shack with a stove was set up beside the pond because there were occasions when a man would misstep and fall into the pond. He would spend some time by the stove while he and his clothes dried out, keeping himself well fortified with rum that was kept on hand for such mishaps. A cold, windy day on the pond could be rough work.

Another seasonal activity, one that took place in the fall, was threshing. I never participated in it for the practice was discontinued when I was a child, but I remember it because it was the only time that I saw horse power used to run a machine. At that time we raised oats to feed the horses, and every fall a threshing crew with a threshing machine came around to thresh the oats. The thresher was a large machine that shook the oats from the stalks as they were fed into it. The oats came pouring out of a spout at which bags were filled, and the straw was spit out from the end of an elevated chute. We furnished the horse and the horsepower rig, which was a tread mill with an uphill slant. When the horse trod the mill it turned a large pulley that must have been three feet or more in diameter. The pulley turned slowly, but when its power was transmitted to a much smaller pulley, enough speed was generated to operate the thresher. The chain that turned the pulley ran so easily that it was activated by the weight of the horse. The poor thing had no choice but to keep treading uphill, which provided steady power. It was like trying to climb a descending escalator.

The following year when the crew came around they had acquired a one cylinder gas engine to take the place of the horse. The horse power machine was never used again. It was shoved into a corner in the basement of the barn and it sat there until the barn burned many years later. The prototypes of those first gas engines, now called one lungers, can be seen at antique engine exhibits. They were also used to run circular saws that sawed firewood into stove lengths, but they did not have much power. They were continually stalling and stopping. They were drawn around the countryside by a horse and wagon.

Sugaring was a seasonal activity that occurred in March and April. Our sugar house was at the back end of our woodlot over a half mile from the house, and it was a busy place during those spring months. Our production of about two hundred gallons of syrup was small, but it required a lot of hard labor. Making

William S. Morse

maple syrup is a serious enterprise today in places such as Vermont. The essentials of making it have not changed over the years, but a lot of the unpleasant work of gathering the sap has been eliminated. The sap from our maples, which were scattered throughout the woodlot, was gathered into a large gathering tank that was on a dray pulled by a pair of horses. The sap from the trees was gathered into large pails which then had to be carried, often on sap yokes, to the tank as it wended its way through the woods. In places the snow was deep, and in the spring it was soft and wet. We were continually sinking into it over the open tops of the rubber boots that we wore. Our bootlegs would be packed with cold, wet snow which was most unpleasant. Our feet would be wet and cold and clammy all season. A heavy run of sap would sometimes necessitate boiling all night, and that was often the most enjoyable part of sugaring. The neighbors would drop in to keep us company, bringing jugs of hard cider and lots of doughnuts and other food, and a night boiling session could turn into quite a party.

One place on the farm where the work was not seasonal was the barn and the cow stable. They demanded several hours of work daily, seven days a week the year around, and I suspect that the stable was the place where many young fellows got their belly full of farming. We were given the chores of cleaning out the manure gutters and pitching hay down from the lofts at an early age; chores which had to be done twice a day, early in the morning and at night.

In time one learned to milk, and as soon as he became fairly proficient at it he was given a small quota of cows to be milked night and morning. At first flush one felt quite elated at participating in doing a man's job, but after the passage of a few weeks he began to realize that learning to milk and letting it be known that he could do so was about the dumbest damned thing that he ever did. From then on he was tied to a cow's tail, figuratively and often quite literally. A cow is an unpredictable creature and has to be handled carefully. Often, when being milked by hand, the calmest of them could get quite edgy. They would try to kick, and end up either with their foot in the milk pail, or else they would kick you in the shin or step on your ankle. Both were painful, but more unpleasant things could happen. They could manifest their uneasiness by switching their tail which was usually loaded with manure and urine, and wiping it across your face or wrapping it around your neck.

Seasonal work, such as haying, had an end that was usually celebrated by a few days of rest and relaxation, but work around the stables had no end. It had to be done morning and night, day in and day out, the year around. There were many things, such as the lure of the city and a paying job, that caused young people to leave those hillside subsistence farms. However, an overflowing manure gutter and a urine soaked cow's tail must have been a big factor in causing them to seek greener pastures.

William S. Morse

Paydirt

There are reports of people who have the first dollar that they earned, and some have been accused of having it framed and hanging it on the wall. I am not in either of those categories, but the memory of my first paying job is still with me. It was a red letter event that occurred the summer after my first year in high school. I was around fourteen years old at the time. Jobs were plentiful. The First World War was in progress and many men of the usual work force were in the army. There was hardly any mechanization in those days, and most of the jobs called for hard manual labor, but that was not anything new to a person who had grown up on a hillside farm.

My first paying job was shoveling gravel in a gravel pit. Automobiles were not particularly plentiful at that time, but the people who owned them were the sort who were able to throw their weight around, and they were beginning to clamor for better roads. The first response of the towns and the state was to start surfacing the most traveled roads with gravel, which was done by men wielding shovels.

Shoveling gravel did not require much intelligence; all one had to do was push a shovel into the bank, load it with gravel, and throw the gravel into a dump cart. Two of the town simpletons were in our crew. They were good workers and could, as one of them put it, "Shubble grabble to beat hell." It was a good thing for them that they could. Sometimes one of them would miss the cart with his shovel full of gravel and it would land on the pit boss who worked close to the cart at the foot of the bank. In spite of the imprecations that he heaped on them, they would think it was funny.

At the time I started working in the pit all of the gravel was hauled by two-horse dump carts, and it was our job to load them. The pit was small and could handle only two carts at a time. As soon as we had them loaded, two more would be waiting to back in. We didn't get much respite. We started shoveling at seven in the morning and worked until the last cart was loaded, which would be between four-thirty and five. Everyone, men and horses, took a full hour break at noon to eat lunch and get a little rest. The pit boss made sure that everyone did his share of the work in getting the carts loaded and out of the pit as soon as possible.

The job was hard on both men and shovels, and when the first trucks began to show up it became hard

on the horses. The teamsters pushed their horses to
their limit trying to beat the trucks. One truck came
on the job near the end of my first summer, but it was
small and turned out to be a nuisance. It would have
a hard time pulling out of the pit with a load, and it
slowed the entire operation. The boss made a special
place where it could be loaded, but it often needed
repairs, and it didn't haul much gravel. The next
summer a couple of heavier trucks came on the job
and they soon proved they could outdo the horses.
Their loads were about the same as the dump carts,
but they made two or three trips to the horse's one.
From then on horse drawn dump carts became fewer
in number, and we had to work a bit harder.

I shoveled gravel for two summers. If we didn't
lose any time because of poor weather and were able to
get in a full week, we received about fifteen dollars.
It doesn't sound like much, but it was all our own.
Nothing was taken out of it for taxes or other
contributions to the government, and it would buy
ten times as much as it would buy today. One could
buy a new outfit, suit, shoes and hat for ten or twelve
dollars.

The last two summers of my high school years
I worked for a horse trader who had turned into a
car dealer. His name was Damon, and I learned
more from him about trading and wheeling and
dealing than could be gleaned from any business
course. During my two years with him I acquired a
fairly good knowledge of the way a horse trader's
mind works, which is something that cannot be
taught in any school. At that time automobiles were
beginning to become fairly numerous in the rural

areas and Damon sold quite a number of them. His main dealership was for the Nash, but different makes of cars were making their debut by the dozen, and Damon grabbed the dealership of all he was able to obtain. He figured that there was safety in numbers, as any one of them might take off and duplicate the success of the Ford. I cannot remember the names of the many different makes of cars which came on the market. The majority of them did not last long.

One make that we handled was the Essex, which was a small Hudson. The Hudson was a large car that became the rum runners' workhorse, but the Essex was smaller. It was quite fast. We used to take it out on the Flats where there was a straight road and get it up to sixty miles an hour which we considered to be quite a stunt. That was fast traveling over the roads of those days. Another car that Damon sold and that did not last long was the Velie. The Velie was quite a nice car, revolutionary in its styling, and I liked it, but it didn't prove to be a success. Many of the cars sold in those days were open touring cars with a top which folded back like a buggy top, but closed sedans were becoming very popular.

My work with Damon varied. I was fairly good with figures and helped him with his bookkeeping. Most of the time I helped unload and assemble cars when they came in. Autos were shipped in freight cars at that time. In order to crowd all of the autos which they could into a freight car, they were often shipped without fenders and running boards which would be stored underneath the chassis. Sometimes we would get only the chassis with the seat and the motor on it, and the body would be stored elsewhere in the freight

car. There was always assembly work waiting to be
done. A barn was our main base of operations. All of
the repair and assembly work was done on the barn
floor.

Often Damon would have me follow him on
his trading forays. He would say: "I'm going out to old
Turner's and sell him a car. Follow me with the Essex
and we'll come back with a note and a mortgage or
some cows." If he got a note we would both ride home
in the Essex. If he had to take two or three cows to
make the trade Damon would drive the Essex home
and I would have to drive the cows. Most of the
people in our area preferred to buy a car either by
paying cash on the barrel head or by making some sort
of a trade. They didn't care for deferred payment plans.
During those early years, and for many years afterwards, most of the cars were sold door to door. A car
salesman would start out with a car and stop at every
place he thought there might be a chance for a sale.

People who owned farms predominated in our
area, and the majority of the sales were made to them.
The farmers didn't know much about a car. They were
used to driving horses hitched to a lumber wagon or a
plow, and they treated a car as if it was a battleship. A
few months after buying a car they would bring it back
to Damon with a knocking motor and a transmission
or a rear end that sounded like a buzz saw. Damon
would trade with them for another car and fix the
one they brought in for sale to another farmer. The
mechanic would fix the motor and fill the transmission or rear end with grease mixed with a liberal
amount of sawdust to quiet them down. Using
sawdust was a usual procedure. The dealers figured

that a farmer would drive the car as if it were a mowing machine, and that new parts wouldn't last any longer than the old ones.

At the start of my third summer in high school I did a short stint working in the pit in the sawmill. It was a hell hole. The pit is at the rear end of the mill where all of the lumber that the mill produces ends up. It was on a lower level than the rest of the mill, and the boards dropped into it after they left the trimmer. It was my job as pitman to sort the boards out as to species, width and length. It was all green lumber and it was heavy.

I could just about keep even with the mill when they were sawing inch boards, but when they started sawing two inch stuff, it was so heavy that I couldn't handle it, and I would get buried in lumber. The sawdust blower was located underneath the mill a short distance from the pit. I found out that I could block it by throwing a piece of trimming into it, and the mill would have to shut down to unblock it. By the time the mill started up again I would have the pit in shape. The mill man began to search for the reason why the blower blocked so often, and I figured I had better quit before he found out.

There was but little mechanization in those days and jobs were quite plentiful. There were no federal or state labor laws restricting kids and young people from working. There were jobs in road building, in the woods and saw mills, and on the farms and in the factories. It seems that performing many of them would be illegal today for young people between fourteen and eighteen years of age. Those jobs were beneficial to a kid. They kept him occupied and out of mischief. A young person learned the discipline of the working place at an early age. Aside from earning money, he learned what he could do and found out what he enjoyed doing. He picked up a true sense of responsibility and independence and a working knowledge of the opportunities that were available to him. He learned that he had to get along with people and adapt himself to their ways.

It was after leaving the pit job in the sawmill that I went to work for Damon. I am glad that I did, for many of the things I learned while working for him proved to be helpful, and even today some of them stand me in good stead. Damon had survived years of trading, and he knew how to handle people and how to achieve his ends. He once told me: "Times and the way things are done are always changing, but people don't change. There are a few smart people, and there are some who think they are smart, and there are a lot of damn fools. A man has to learn to sort them out and handle them before he gets anywhere."

Gramp

During my childhood and boyhood years there were times when my grandfather lived with us. He was my maternal grandfather, and the farm on which we lived used to belong to him. When my grandmother died he sold the farm to my father. He often had interests which called for his presence elsewhere, but until he died he made the farm his home and his headquarters. When I was a child I didn't know if we lived with him or if he lived with us.

I do not know anything of his ancestors. My mother and her brothers said that his family came from Canada. I have not been able to find any record of him in any of the nearby towns, and it is evident

that he did not spring from any of the old time settlers
of our area as my father did. He used to be a cooper,
making wooden barrels, tubs, buckets and containers
of all sorts until the wide use of metal rendered them
obsolete. He could make almost anything out of wood,
and continued working with it off and on while I was a
boy.

He had a shop at one end of the carriage shed
which was full of hand tools and various foot and
hand operated devices that were used before power
tools became available. The shop was a fascinating
place to a boy, and some of the things my grandfather
made were interesting. He occasionally made buggy
whips for people who wanted something better and
different than those sold by the trade. In those horse
and buggy days one of a man's treasured possessions
was his buggy whip. There were some who were
willing to pay the extra money that my grandfather
charged to make them. He made them out of ash or
hickory and leather. They had decorated handles, and
each one was distinctive.

There were times when my grandfather carried
on a business making ladder rounds. At that time
ladders were made of wood, and the ladder rounds
were hand made. Each round was individually shaved
out of a square piece of oak by a man pulling a large
spoke shave. The square stock was held in a chest high
foot operated vise called a "horse," and the spoke
shave was shaped so that it formed the round. It took
a lot of muscle to pull the shave, but there were men
who could turn out a thousand rounds a day. My
grandfather used to contract to produce them in car
load lots, and at times he would have a number of

A Country Life

people around the countryside shaving rounds for him. I was too young to have enough muscle to shave rounds, but I learned how to produce the square stock by froeing it out of a block of oak with a froe and a mallet.

I was an only child with no brothers or sisters to play or fight with, and there were many times when my grandfather provided me with the only companionship that I had. When he was working in his shop, he would find something for me to do that would give me a sense of helping him. Evenings he would join me when I had studying to do. He had a way of making a game of everything, even when we peeled apples.

He was a herbist with a belief in many of the old time remedies, and I often accompanied him when he searched for herbs in the woods. I learned that steeped sweet fern was good for poison ivy, and that wintergreen tea was a pleasant drink before going to bed. Some of the things that he cooked up from herbs smelled and tasted so horrible that the dog would shrink from them. Every summer he lined bees searching for a bee tree for a winter's supply of honey. Lining bees was fun, but robbing them of their store of honey could be painful.

His roots may have been in Canada, but he had all of the traits of a Yankee trader. Trading was sort of a pastime with him, and he was always coming home with something that he had obtained in a trade. I never knew of his doing it in excess, but he liked to tipple once in a while, and when he mixed tippling and trading he often came home with some strange things. I will never forget the time he came home from one of his trading forays with a half-dozen geese.

One of my chores was taking care of the hens and our other poultry. The geese were added to my flock, and I soon began to rue the day that my grandfather brought them home. Those geese must have been among the most pernicious creatures that were ever created. They seemed to have a strong dislike of everybody. They would bite the hand that fed them, and from the start there was a state of war between them and everyone on the farm. They would plot to lurk and waylay a person and bite him at every opportunity, and then run off honking in derision.

Geese are very large birds. They are primarily grass and vegetation feeders, and they are endowed with large strong beaks that enable them to get a firm grip on whatever they want to pull out of the ground. When they bite a person on the calf or his buttocks it hurts. Visitors learned to approach the house warily whenever the geese were around. Those which my grandfather had traded for were about as bad as a vicious dog, and we had to get rid of them. We tried eating a couple of them, but as I recall they were pretty poor fare. When I die and go to whatever place I am destined for, I hope it is one where there are no geese.

My grandfather never engaged in horse trading. He called it a deceitful business. He usually tried to dicker for something that was of some practical or commercial use. He ushered us into the motor age by trading a woodlot for a Model T Ford – a trade that he regretted making the first time he tried to start the thing. The old automobiles were started by standing in front of them and spinning the motor with a crank, and in doing so with the old Model T a person was in a ticklish position. Even when the transmission was locked into neutral some of them had a tendency to advance on a person as soon as the motor started.

The advance was not violent – E. B. White likened it to a horse nudging someone for an apple – but it was persistent. My grandfather tried to hold the car back by pushing against it, but it kept working him backwards towards a woodpile that was in the yard. He couldn't escape from it, and he started swearing and yelling "whoa," but the car didn't stop until the motor misfired and died. Even after he learned to drive it, he steered clear of cranking the car if there was someone around who would do it for him.

A few years before the first World War he began engaging in various small business ventures. He owned creameries in the Baker River Valley and Plymouth, which he operated with his two sons. After the war he sold out to Hood and bought a laundry that he ran for a while before selling it. He continued buying and selling various small enterprises until he died. To him I guess it was another form of trading. He never believed in working for anyone, and he often tried to impress me with his philosophy by telling me to learn to skin my own skunks instead of skinning those that belong to someone else.

William S. Morse

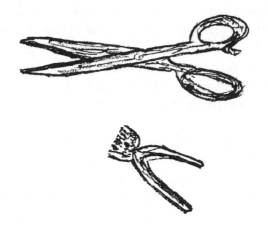

Mom

My mother was the good Samaritan of our district and was always ready to help those in distress. People also looked to her to provide some of the services that were not available in our area of hillside farms. One of them was cutting hair. The nearest barber was in the next village which was six or seven miles distant from us. Getting a haircut from him was a time consuming process. Those who were fortunate enough to have electricity in those early days could only use it for lighting purposes; there were no appliances. The tools which our barber used were hand clippers and shears, and he was a slow moving person. He would stop cutting hair and hold forth for several minutes on any subject that was either dear or obnoxious to him. He chewed tobacco, and it would take him three or four minutes to go to the spittoon and unload. If travel time was counted, getting a haircut from him spoiled almost a day.

It was ten or twelve miles to the nearest doctor, and the two or three hours that it would take for old Dobbin to reach him was too long a time when an emergency arose. The people of the district often turned to my mother to patch up minor injuries in addition to serving as a barber.

Unless a person had some special reason, such as attending a funeral or a wedding or visiting the city, getting a haircut was not a very pressing matter. Some people got pretty shaggy before visiting her, and my mother earned whatever she got from them for doing the chore. One person who lived near the foot of the mountain would let his hair and beard grow for a year. A haircut and a shave once a year was a spring ritual with him, and doing the job was about the same as that of shearing a sheep. He used to take the train to Woodsville and have one of the barbers there do the chore, but after a while they refused to have anything to do with him, and my mother won the job by default.

Except for his hair he was not unkempt; he was clean and decent. His hair and beard were coal black, and by the time they had grown for a year his eyes and the tip of his nose were the only features of his face that could be seen. He looked like a shaggy bear, and was about as frightful as one. My mother would use the horse clippers on him and cut his hair and beard as close as she could, but she refused to shave him. She would make him go over to the kitchen sink and shave himself. He would use my father's razor which made my father mad. Ed's beard was so tough that it would almost ruin a razor. After his haircut and shave people could get a glimpse of what he really looked like. His dog bit him once because he didn't recognize him.

Ed was the worst specimen that my mother had to contend with, but there were some who ran him a close second. Most of the people came around in the evening to get their haircut, and it was often a social event during which a pitcher of cider might be consumed. It beat going to a barber shop. Our district was sparsely settled. I cannot recall more than eighteen or twenty families within an area of several square miles. Cutting people's hair was not a frequent occurrence, and my mother did it more as a matter of accommodation than anything else.

My mother's medical duties were mostly confined to patching cuts and bruises. The most frequent jobs were axe cuts. If they were real bad she would bandage them up and stop them from bleeding badly until a doctor could attend to them. A druggist in Woodsville was a family friend, and he furnished my mother with the medical supplies and placebos that he thought she might need. Her biggest headache was an old lady who lived a short distance from us. Her husband made ends meet by cutting firewood for people who lived in the village. She was a small, wizened up old woman who smoked an old blackened clay pipe which had a broken stem. The part of the stem that remained was so short that the bowl of the pipe was practically under her nose, and she was seldom seen without the pipe in her mouth.

A Country Life

Somewhere along her life's way she had become addicted to dope. Dope addiction was a rarity in those days, especially in our area, and she was up against it in obtaining the stuff when she needed it. She would come over to see my mother when she was almost crazy for relief, and she was an object of pity. My mother told our druggist friend about her condition, and he gave her some morphine or cocaine to dole out to the old lady when she was badly in need of it. From then on it was a tug of war between her and my mother, and it was a relief to us when they moved away.

I happened to be around when she once had to do an emergency job on Ed, the one who sported long hair. He had been chopping wood, and he came to my mother with a large and long ugly sliver of wood that was driven entirely through his hand at the fleshy base of his thumb. My mother tried to have him let one of us drive him to the doctor, but he insisted that she take it out. She got my father's razor and produced a bottle of whiskey that she kept hidden away for emergencies. Ed nibbled away at the whiskey while he watched her cut the sliver out. Both he and the whiskey must have been of sterling quality, for he never flinched. After cutting the sliver out she washed the wound with whiskey and bandaged it. He claimed that it healed perfectly and never troubled him. I can remember watching the operation and deciding not to be a doctor.

Aside from doling out toothache wax, my mother refused to have anything to do with teeth. A farmer named Homer, who was reputed to be the tightest miser in the county, lived some distance from us. He once came to my mother and tried to get her to pull a tooth which was troubling him. She refused and told him to go to a dentist. We found out later that Homer had already been to one. His tooth had a gold filling, and it had been bothering him for some time. He had visited a dentist in Woodsville and tried to get him to pull it for the gold filling that was in the tooth. The dentist refused the deal, and told Homer that he charged money to pull a tooth. Homer didn't want to part with any money, and he told the dentist that he guessed he would let her hum a while longer. The tooth evidently got to humming much louder, and Homer tried to inveigle my mother into pulling it.

My mother never reaped any great benefits from the services which she rendered, and she never expected any. She was concerned with the people's welfare and their well being. The things which she did to help people out would probably be considered of small account today, but at that time the district would have been a much poorer place to live without her presence.

Food

One thing can be said of the people who gained their living from subsistence farms in rural New England in the early years of the century: they ate well. Their fare was plain and simple, but it is one of the few things of that era which I can recall with a sense of nostalgia.

William S. Morse

Like many of the farm activities their food varied with the seasons, and was dependent upon what they produced or were able to obtain through the generosity of nature. There were no supermarkets or any of the modern marvels of food preservation such as electric refrigerators or freezers, but people managed well without them. The items that could not be raised on the farm were purchased or obtained by trade from the general store. People did not buy hand to mouth. My parents purchased flour, sugar, and crackers by the barrel; tea by the chest; and coffee beans by the bag. Those items, along with salt and pepper and a few spices, were all that were needed; more likely, they were all we could afford.

We did not have the variety of food that is available today. The food that was indigenous and acclimated to the area was our only fare at that time. Things from distant places, such as oranges and bananas, were rare and strange to us. Bananas were called monkey food. One of my uncles said that he started to eat his first banana without peeling it.

People took all that nature had to offer. After a winter's diet of meat and cellar stored vegetables they jumped avidly upon the first greens of spring, such as dandelions and fiddleheads. They dug and consumed them by the bushel. It sounds like pretty poor pickings, but right now I would relish a meal of boiled dandelions and potatoes with salt pork and gravy. Today dandelions and fiddleheads are considered to be gourmet foods.

Another spring addition to our diet was freshly caught fish. That was before automobiles gave people ready access to our streams, and fish were abundant.

A Country Life

The north branch of the Oliverian was a short distance from our house and it teemed with trout. When my mother planned for a meal of fish she would give me a large lard pail and tell me to go down to the brook and get some fish. I would be back in a little over an hour with a pail full of trout, running ten or twelve inches or more in length – enough for a good meal for the family. Evenings we would go to the mill pond, and by the light of a lantern or a bonfire we would catch so many horned pout that we would give half of them away to our neighbors. We were not purists; we used worms for bait. Although we had fun, we were not fishing for sport. We were after food.

Practically everyone had large gardens that added to their summer fare, but the largest share of the garden harvest was canned or preserved for winter use by storing it in the cellar. Before the installation of central heat spoiled them for food storage, those old cellars played a very important role in the food chain. They were tailored for the job, with dirt floors and walls of large stone blocks. Some had a well in them. Our cellar had a small stream running through it. They were deep and dark with a little ventilation at the top, and the result was a winter atmosphere that hovered just above the freezing mark with enough humidity to keep fruit and vegetables palatable throughout the winter. By late fall the cellar was a storehouse of food with barrels and boxes of apples and potatoes, shelves of canned garden produce and root vegetables, crocks of salt pork in brine, smoked hams and bacon hanging from the joists – and barrels of cider.

Cider was an important product of the farm and

was given loving care and attention. Every farm had its small apple orchard. Some of the apples were stored for eating and cooking purposes, but the largest share of the crop was pressed into apple juice and aged in the cellar until it became hard cider. It had its uses which were mainly for social purposes. A family possessing a cellar that made good cider did not have to worry about being lonesome.

Our meat supply came from animals that were raised and fed for that purpose. Except for hams and bacon, which were cured and smoked, the meat required cold and freezing weather to keep through the winter. Its preparation had to wait for the advent of sufficiently cold weather, which became our butchering season. It usually occurred around the first of December, and took place at a spot reserved for it that had a brick arch with a large iron kettle for heating water. Close to the arch were two high uprights with a cross beam on which to hang the carcasses.

The place had a good workout during the deer season, which took place in November. We lived in good game country, and for three or four weeks our farm, and also a cousin's farm that was nearby, took on the aspect of a sporting camp. We had a steady and paying clientele from Lowell and Boston who came up to hunt the area. They were experienced hunters, and there were usually two or three deer and occasionally a bear hanging from the cross beam. Most of the hunters got their quota, which at that time was two deer for the season. They would pack the meat that they took home with them in ice, and return down country on the train. Hunting season was a spirited and lively occasion. While it lasted we had venison coming out of our ears. If the weather was cold enough, we would be able to freeze some of it for our use in the winter months; otherwise, my mother would make mincemeat of it, the real old style mincemeat, made with venison and cider.

After the excitement of the hunting season, butchering would have been a dull event if it hadn't been for Herb. Herb lived on a small place about a quarter of a mile up the road from us, and was our next door neighbor. He did all of our butchering, and he went at it with a gusto that made it sort of a special occasion, especially when he slaughtered a hog. It was Herb's belief that the only way to get good meat from a hog was to stick him with a knife and let him bleed to death, which necessitated getting into the pen and cornering the animal. If you have never seen a man in a pen that is slippery with mud and excrement, doing battle with a two hundred pound hog you have missed something. For a few minutes the action was fast and furious, and there were times when it was hard to tell which was Herb and which was the hog. Stamina wise the hog was in pretty poor shape, as he had been heavily fed for some weeks to prepare him for the table. His staying power was limited, and it didn't take Herb very long to poop him and deliver the fatal blow.

The hog was then quickly toted to the arch where he was hung to the cross beam head down over a hogshead of scalding water, into which he was lowered several times while the hair was shaved from his hide by a process called candling; so called because the device used to shave him with was shaped exactly

like a candlestick. It had a razor sharp base that shaved
the hog cleanly, and when it had been shaved and
washed it hung from the cross beam as white as snow.

Slaughtering a beef animal was not as exciting as
killing the hog. Bleeding it was not as critical, and it
was usually shot. It was skinned instead of shaved. A
hog furnished a greater variety of meat. Its hams and
bacon were cured and smoked, and they would keep
for a long time. The fat belly strips were immersed in
salt brine and became salt pork. Hog's head cheese was
made of the head meat, and everything else, except
for the chops, was made into sausage. The hog even
provided toys for us when we were kids. Its bladder
was dried and then blown up, providing us with a ball
which took an astounding amount of punishment. It
could be kicked and batted around the house for the
balance of the winter, and for many kids it was the first
thing in the shape of a ball that they saw. I don't know
how he did it, but my grandfather used to make a
whistle for me out of the hog's curly tail. A hog can
be a very productive animal.

The beef quarters and the balance of the hog that
wasn't processed were placed on a plank table in one
of the unheated rooms of the house – usually a back
bedroom – where they froze and became our meat
larder for the winter.

The hens and other poultry that we raised were
the only sure source of fresh meat available to us the
year around. We raised them for egg production, but
there were always several that had stopped laying, and
they were slated for the table whenever we wanted
one. I became convinced that those hens had extra-
sensory perception. They seemed to be aware of their

A Country Life

fate. When we set out to catch one of them we had a worse time snaring it than Herb had cornering the hog. Those hens were much different than the bland tasting chickens that are offered in today's supermarkets. They were older, and had spent their lives running free around the farm yard feeding on scraps and bugs, and they acquired a flavor which was all their own. They were old and they were tough, and I guess that they had to be cooked a long time to make them tender, but when you opened up a chicken pie with gravy and dumplings made of one of them you had something pretty special that is hard to obtain today.

All of our food was cooked and prepared in her kitchen by my mother. There were no processed foods available. We could not have a change of fare by going out to eat, for there were no restaurants or fast food joints. The larger towns had hotels which served meals, but the nearest one was fifteen miles away which was too long a jaunt for old Dobbin. The only chance people had for a change was when the Grange or the Church put on a feed. They were well attended, especially the church suppers. There would be twice as many people at a church supper than there were at Sunday services, which I suppose proves that a man's stomach takes precedence over his soul.

People had never heard of calories or cholesterol and they must have consumed enormous amounts of them. Their diets would probably drive today's dietitians to distraction. The hard work which they did must have overcome the ill effects of their excesses, for most of them lived to a fairly ripe old age. Taking everything into consideration, people probably eat better today than they did in those early years. They

William S. Morse

have access to a greater variety of food that is processed in ways that were beyond the imagination in those early days. However, I feel that those of us who lived on subsistence farms in the first decades of the century had one big advantage that the people of today do not enjoy. We knew what we were eating, and we knew where it came from. It was our food that was on the table.

Cyder

Historians tell us that apple trees were not native to this country. Their dates are confusing, but it seems that the first apple trees were brought from England a few years after the Pilgrims landed at Plymouth, and that the first orchard in New England was planted in Boston before 1630. The trees quickly spread by propagation and by escaping to the forests where they grew wild. One hundred and fifty years later, in 1773, they were in such abundance that James Whitelaw, while traveling down the lower Connecticut river, made the following observation in his account of the trip: "...it is not uncommon for one farmer to make one hundred barrels of cyder in one year..." That is a lot of cyder!

Reports can be found of much greater production, but they smack more of boasting than of reliable

reporting. Whitelaw was returning down river to
Hartford after viewing the town of Ryegate, a large part
of which he purchased for a company of Scotch settlers.
We can accept his account as fairly correct for he was a
man of excellent repute who later became Surveyor
General of Vermont.

At the time the Pilgrims and Puritans made
their pitch in the New World, beer was the preferred
drink in England, and they brought it along with
them. That was how John Alden made it aboard the
Mayflower. He was a cooper who the Pilgrims hired to
look after their water and beer barrels. It had to take
some time for the first apple trees to mature and bear
fruit enough to produce cider in any quantity, but
when they did, cider gradually replaced beer as the
everyday drink.

According to the records and writings of those
seventeenth and eighteenth century years, everyone,
men, women and children drank it. It was a product of
the soil, and they served it with their daily meals. The
large landed estates had their own cider presses, and
cider mills sprang up to take care of the farmers who
had smaller orchards. Cider was cheap. It made its
way to the taverns, and it seems that an incredible
amount of it was consumed.

John Adams once stated that taverns were
too numerous, and that in most country towns in
this country almost every other house had a sign of
entertainment before it. He evidently made good use
of them as he rode his circuits, for he is reported to
have later said that it was in listening to the tavern
talks among farmers that he first came to realize that
American independence was both inevitable and close

at hand. There was a drink in those days comprised of a mixture of cider and rum which was called a stonewall. A few of those making their rounds must have made a tavern a good political sounding board.

The southern part of New England – Massachusetts, Connecticut and southern New Hampshire – was the thickly settled area of Adam's and Whitelaw's time. The upper Connecticut valley and the country east and west of it were either empty or receiving their first settlers. The burden and labor of settling what was then a wilderness were probably eased by rum as it was easily transported. However, after the orchards which they planted began to bear fruit, cider became an important product of the farms, and it probably flowed as freely as it had down river.

My ancestors settled in the foothills of the upper Connecticut valley, and in the first two decades of this century I spent my boyhood and young manhood there living in an area of hillside subsistence farms. Cider flowed freely at that time, and it was as common as meat and potatoes. Every farm had its orchard, and every village had its cider mill which pressed the apples into apple juice. Barrels of the juice were stored in the cellar where they were nursed as they turned into hard cider.

Production per farm was small. It varied according to the size of its orchard and the thirst of its occupants. Except for the prohibition years, I can not recall any commercial production. One might sell a little cider as a favor, but the primary use of its production was for home consumption.

Our orchard was small. I guess that we made about six to eight barrels each year. It did not all end

up as hard cider, for there were other uses for it. A self
sufficient farm required a lot of vinegar, and at least
one barrel was allowed to acidify. The vinegar which
my father made was much more potent than the
diluted stuff which is on the market today; it would
knock your hat off. When my mother made pickles
the aroma of the vinegar would advertise the fact well
down the road.

The quality of the cider varied according to the
cellar in which it was aged. One never heard of bad
cider, but some cellars made much better cider than
others. A knowledgeable person could drink a glass of
it and tell whose cellar it came from. My father and
grandfather were very fussy with their cider. They
would rack it off one or two times into clean barrels
before they bunged it tight to age. Cider pressed in
the fall would be about right to bung tight around
February, and when it had aged a year or so it would be
a top notch product ready for use. The process took
time.

Hard cider, by itself, has a low alcoholic content.
It was standard procedure to increase its potency by
adding all sorts of stuff to it as it fermented. Sugar,
often in the form of honey or maple syrup, was the
most common and effective addition, but there were
all sorts of recipes; some of them were weird. Raisins,
corn, beets, chokecherries and other berries were often
added. One of our neighbors put beefsteak in his
barrels. My grandfather was not immune to the
practice, but his recipe made some sense. He always
reserved one barrel to which he added rock candy and
a generous amount of brandy before he bunged it.
That barrel was supposed to be used for special

occasions, but it was usually empty before the following year's press was ready to be tapped.

Tinkering with the cider hurried it along and increased its muscle, but most of the ingredients that were added lowered its quality. To make good hard cider the process has to be left pretty much to its own devices and given one to two years to age. There were always two, and sometimes three, presses each in a different stage of fermenting and aging stored in the cellar. It required a lot of barrels to keep the process going.

The knowledge that a person had good cider in his cellar could create a nuisance. A man named Joe had a small farm a mile up the road from us. He had a propensity for the juice, and some evenings he would harness Banner, his horse, and set out to do a little carousing. Upon his return home in the late hours of the evening when we were asleep, he would drive Banner into our yard, wake us up, and try to cadge some cider. My father would stick his head out of the window and berate the hell out of him until he went home. However, Joe was a devious character. The next morning, on his way to the creamery, he would always stop and apologize profusely for disturbing us, but while making the apology he would usually manage to cadge a glass or two of cider.

Naturally aged cider is a mild and pleasant drink; almost every one drank it. It was a matter of sociability to draw a pitcher from the cellar whenever one had visitors. Some of the elderly emulated John Adams and had it at breakfast. They drank it as we drink orange juice today. It was supposed to be healthful. It seems that cider was always considered to have medicinal value. Even in my time some doctors prescribed it on occasions. It was a standard cold remedy. Our family remedy was a piping hot mug of cider into which a generous amount of ginger and a bit of cinnamon had been mulled. I do not know how effective it was as a cure, but I can testify that it greatly eased the misery of having a cold.

A drink called applejack could be made of hard cider, but no one in our area made it as it was considered to be wasteful of good cider. A cousin and I tried making some as an experiment. My grandfather, who used to be a cooper, made us a ten gallon barrel that he called a firkin. We filled it with hard cider and left it outdoors all winter. We tapped it in the spring before it had a chance to thaw, and were disgusted to find that we had less than a gallon of applejack. The shrinkage was terrific, but the product was chain lightning. It was a durable drink. If one drank enough during an evening to get a jag on, a couple of glasses of water the next morning would set it off again.

One would have to go back to the early years of the century and live the life of a countryman of that time to appreciate the benign uses of cider. During haying season in the summer my father kept a couple of jugs of it cooling in the icehouse. After toiling in the hot sun pitching on a load of hay, and then wrestling with it while storing it in the lofts of a hot, dusty, airless barn, a glass of cold cider refreshed one's spirit, and made the prospect of returning to the field for another load more bearable.

In the winter, after a day working outside in the cold and the wind, a mug or two of hot cider helped drive the chill from one's bones. It had uses that were more salubrious than that of wassail.

The custom of making cider as it was widely done in the bygone days has disappeared. The urbanization of the country which, even in the rural areas, enables people to meet their needs by purchasing instead of producing, has probably been the major factor contributing to its demise. Today cider is made by some wineries and is sold in various forms ranging from draft cider of low alcoholic content to apple wine and brandy, which are stronger. Orchardists press a large amount of apple juice that is sold the year around as sweet cider. Some of them put up a barrel or so to age for their own use, but those whom I have talked with have no knowledge of anyone else doing so. The old cider barrels and their home made product are relics of the distant past, along with the horse and buggy and the privy.

William S. Morse

Privy Matters

Charles "Chic" Sale wrote the classic treatise on privies – *The Specialist* – quite a few years ago. He wrote as a person whose lifelong ambition and profession was the building of privies, at which he considered himself a success. In reading his account of privies one became quite knowledgeable about the architectural details of their construction.

Chic Sale wrote of the proper distance from the house to locate them: far enough away so that they

A Country Life

were not objectionable, and yet close enough so
that they could be reached quickly in case of a dire
emergency. He wrote of the benefit of orienting them
so that one could leave the door open and bask in the
sun while performing his duties, if one found it restful
to do so. He emphasized the importance of having the
number of holes related to the size of the family that
was to use it, and pointed out the advantage of locating
it near the woodpile so that people could lug an armful
of wood into the house upon their return from their
visit to it. He detailed the process of anchoring it
securely, and even covered the decorations on the
door. In reading his account, one became aware of the
fact that at some time in the past people must have
spent a lot of time sitting in privies.

 As I recall, Sale did not name the locale in
which his privies graced the countryside, but it must
have been some place other than New England. The
privies that he described were single structures located
a short distance from the house which they served,
and they stood alone. They were entities in themselves. Perhaps his builder operated in the mid-west.
In most of the old New England farmhouses that I
have known a different style was practiced.

 When our forebears built their houses they had
an eye for comfort, and they placed their privies within
the perimeters of the house itself, usually at the far end
of the woodshed. Like Sale's privies, it was quite a few
steps from the comfort of the living quarters of the
house. The shed was unheated and received hardly
any sunshine, but one did not have to face the ordeal
of hightailing through a New England blizzard when
matters were urgent. It also met the requirement of

being near the supply of firewood, and in a busy household, that went a long way towards keeping the kitchen woodbox filled.

Placing the privy in the woodshed also kept it from suffering the adversity caused by pranksters. A person named Tracey, who lived in the village, had a free standing privy outside of his house. Each Fourth of July and Halloween the boys used to tip it over. It was the only free standing privy in the area, and they almost wore it out. The prank didn't seem to bother Tracey much as the privy was a small two holer, and it wasn't much of a chore to set it upright again. One Fourth of July eve the boys changed their routine, and toted the privy over to the small common near the store where they ran it up the flagpole. The episode provoked Tracey into building a new privy attached to his shed, which deprived the boys of any more fun with him.

The prank aroused some envy in the adjoining villages, which were quite competitive with each other in those years. The following Fourth of July the boys in Haverhill took a free standing privy from Ladd Street and placed it on the railroad track. The first train down early the next morning was the milk run, and the engineer said that he almost dropped his teeth when he came around the curve and his headlight picked up the privy in the center of the tracks. There wasn't anything he could do to change the situation, so he pulled down the Johnson Bar and ducked his head inside the cab. He inspected his engine at the next stop, and found that one of the holes in the privy seat had made a ringer over one of the small flagstaffs that were on each side of the cowcatcher. For some time afterwards he left the seat there as a memento, and the run became locally known as the two holer instead of the milk train.

A privy within the shed, or attached to it, could not be tipped over, but it was not entirely immune from pranksters. As a rule, the bottom part of the privy was not sheathed over. It was left open for ventilation, and for access to clean it out. The opening was large enough for the insertion of a good-sized hornet's nest if the boys were able to obtain one. It was a good idea for a person to give his privy a thorough inspection before using it on Fourth of July morning.

All of the privies that I ever saw were quite crude affairs. They were small and of unfinished rough construction. They were no place to dawdle, although Bertha Damon in her book, *A Sense of Humus*, described one which was quite fancy. It was whitewashed with pictures on the wall, a rug on the floor and a nail keg that served as a small table to hold magazines. She wrote that it was in the ancestral home of a friend, who said she had fixed it up when she was a girl because it was the only quiet place she could find where she could seriously sit and read.

The only thing of finish quality that I ever saw in a privy was the seat. It was a wide, smooth board with three or four holes cut into it. There was usually a small sized hole meant for children; one or two holes of medium size; and almost always one large one, tailored for those who possessed more ample posteriors. Years of use had given them a patina and a smooth polish which made them fairly comfortable to sit upon.

My father said that when he was a young lad he

William S. Morse

once worked on a large farm, where the farmer intentionally roughed up his privy seats to such an extent that it was almost torture to sit on them. He said that the farmer was an old skinflint, and that he roughed up his privy holes so that his hired help would not waste their time and his money sitting in the privy any longer than was necessary.

I never knew of a house with more than one privy, but a friend of mine told me of one that had four of them. He said that when he was a boy, in the eighteen nineties, his mother ran a boarding house in Lebanon that was named The Rising Sun. He described the house as a large four story one, which had a privy on every floor. Sometime later, in thinking about it, I tried to imagine what a four story privy could be like. Each privy must have been cantilevered over the one beneath it. The fourth story one had to be subject to a pretty strong draft, and it must have had quite a drop. There were people in those days who made the cleaning out of privies their principal occupation. They must have approached the chore of cleaning out that four story one with quite a degree of apprehension. It could have been quite hazardous, working directly underneath three privies, with a likely chance of being bombed.

One of the strangest experiences of my life involved a privy. The incident occurred during the early nineteen thirties at the height, or rather the depth, of the depression. Roosevelt was doing all that he could to provide jobs, and one of the government projects was a survey of the rural areas of the country. I hooked on with the Grafton County Farm Bureau to do the southern part of the County. The project involved visiting each rural family unit and farm, and filling out a long questionnaire.

One summer afternoon I was doing Center Holderness, and my last call was at a farmhouse that had a long porch along the side of the house. I was in a hurry to finish work for the day, and did not take much notice of the surroundings. I went upon one corner of the porch and knocked on what I supposed was the kitchen door. I had knocked several times without getting any response, when a voice from behind me inquired as to what I wanted.

I turned around, and discovered that on the other end of the porch there was a privy. The door was open, and a rather elderly gentleman with a white mustache was sitting on the privy seat. He had an old hat on his head, and he was in his undershirt. His trousers and suspenders were down around his ankles, and there was little doubt about the activity that he was engaged in. I explained my mission, stating that it would take some time to complete. He pointed to an old chair that was on the porch, saying if I would bring it closer to him he would try to take care of me. I pulled the chair into a position directly in front of the privy door, and for over a half hour I sat facing him and plying him with questions, which he answered while sitting on the privy seat. He was still sitting there when I made my departure. I have to rate it as the strangest interview which I ever made, and I often think of the old gentleman and his relaxed manner.

There are instances where the privy has become something besides an object of derision. The town of Ashford, Connecticut has what was once a girls' academy dating back to 1825. Its three hole privy has

William S. Morse

been restored. The complex has been placed on the
National Register of Historical Places, and I have
recently read that it is about to become a museum.
A friend of mine, Bob Averill, once worked on the
Appalachian Trail, and one of his privies, which
was quite fancy and attractive, made the National
Geographic Magazine. So, the privy is being
recognized as part of our national heritage, and
also as something that still has a functional value.

Many of the old farmhouses in the rural
sections of northern New England were dependent
upon privies until well into the nineteen thirties.
An ample supply of water was a big problem in many
areas, and indoor plumbing had to wait for the arrival
of electricity, which was slow in reaching a lot of the
rural places. The old privies are still in evidence in a
few of the old farmhouses today, but their busy days
are over, and they are silent sentinels of the distant
past.

Horses

"If wishes were horses the beggars might ride. If horse droppings were crackers they'd eat 'til they died." That was a doggerel that I can remember hearing my grandfather recite quite often. He seemed to find occasions when he felt that it was applicable. In the first two decades of the century, before they began to be pushed aside by the automobile, horses were important in the scheme of rural life. There were no buses then, or any other form of local transportation, and if a man did not own a horse, he and his family had to walk. It was mandatory for a traveler to give a lift to a person who was afoot, and it was as much an act of pity as anything else. Living was geared around the horse. There was usually an empty stall in the stable in which a visitor's horse could be tied and fed. If the hired man owned a horse, its feed and a stall were taken for granted as a part of his wages. Every sizable village had a livery stable that rented horses and rigs to those who had need of them to travel the countryside.

A horse gave a person or a family some status. It might not be any more than a bag of bones, but they could ride instead of having to plod the roads in dust or snow. If a stranger appeared in the area the first thing to receive any notice was his horse and his rig. If they appeared to be smart, then the man himself was accorded some attention. Strangers were always an object of speculation. Every horse and every rig in the neighboring countryside, including those of the doctor and the banker, were well known by everyone. The doctor's appearance would be worrisome, for it meant that someone in the neighborhood was sick. Bankers had a habit in those days of visiting places on which they held a mortgage, and their presence was not considered unusual. If a stranger and his rig passed along the road you began to wonder who he was and where he was going and what he was doing in the neighborhood. The man himself would usually be aware that he was under scrutiny, and if you were handy to the roadside he might stop to pass the time of day and make himself and his errand known.

It was a good idea for a stranger in a place to be on his toes, for people were not averse to pulling his leg and being a little facetious with him. I remember an occasion when I was with my father returning

A Country Life

home from a trip to the creamery. It was mainly uphill from the village to our farm, and there was a strange rig pulled off to the side of the road about half way up the first long hill. There was a man and a woman in it, and they seemed to be arguing. As we pulled alongside we stopped and my father asked if they were having any trouble.

"I God, yes," the man said. "I'm looking for my brother's place.* Can you tell me where he lives?"

"You're going in the wrong direction," my father replied. "You have to turn around and go back to the store and then go east along the flat for a mile or so."

The man expressed his thanks and we proceeded towards home. At the top of the hill I looked back and saw that they had turned around and were headed for the village. I mentioned that I had never seen those people before and asked who they were.

"Damned if I know," my father said. "I never saw them before either. I think they're lost."

I pointed out that he was not of much help to them.

"No," he said, "but they asked sort of a foolish question. They don't seem to be over bright anyhow, and they are probably used to being cogged."

Some people became greatly attached to their horses and kept them until they died. Others considered themselves smart and would trade horses or anything else at the drop of a hat. One such character lived beyond us near the foot of the mountain. He was

---

* "I God" – "I swan" – "I van" were common old Yankee expressions. Some oldtimers started every other sentence with one of them!

76

about as shiftless and worthless as they come. He had
a cow and a horse and a few hens. People wondered
how his animals lived through the cold winters, for
you could throw a cat anywhere through the holes of
his barn, but they survived and so did old Lewis. He
never worked anywhere and he seemed to get along by
trading. He used to drive past our place on his way
home with his wagon loaded with things that he had
picked up. My father said that he stole half of it, but I
never heard of his being caught at it. He acquired a
phonograph which he called a talking machine. It was
the first one in our neighborhood. Evenings we used
to go up to his place to listen to it. It had cylinders for
records and a big morning glory horn that must have
been twenty inches across at the top. He had about
six records, and I guess that we wore them out. I
remember two of Caruso's and one of Harry Lauder's.
Our favorite was one called "The Preacher and the
Bear." Phil Harris resurrected it in the 1940's or the
1950's and it was a big hit.

Old Lewis never drove anything but a wreck of a
horse. I guess he wanted people to feel sorry for him.
He traded horses quite often, and he had some trick of
rejuvenating them just before he traded that made
them look as if they were something. You could tell
when Lewis was planning to trade, for his old wreck
would begin to blossom. My father claimed that he fed
them arsenic. He said that you could start feeding an
old bag of bones a little arsenic, increasing the dose bit
by bit, and soon have him fleshed out and looking like
a new horse. The catch was that when you stopped
feeding him the arsenic the horse quickly reverted back
to an old bag of bones or, more likely, he died. It may

have been so. I can remember one time when Lewis stopped at our place to show off a new horse that he had just obtained in a trade. He liked to brag about his trading prowess. The next morning he went out to the barn to feed him and the horse was dead. My father and grandfather thought it was a huge joke. Someone had beat old Lewis at his own trick by trading him a horse that had been fed arsenic.

There was a period when I was a kid during which we had horses coming out of our ears. A farm had to have horses. My father had two teams of heavy work horses that he used in the woods in the fall and winter, and worked on the farm during spring and summer. We also usually had one horse which served both as a driving horse and a light work horse. My grandfather had a half-brother, our Uncle George, who lived in Medford. At that time one of the leading department stores in Boston was Houghton and Dutton. Mr. Dutton, one of the owners, had a large farm in Medford. He was a great horseman, and Uncle George was his head wrangler. If they had some horses that they wanted to get rid of, they never traded them or sent them to the glue factory; they loaded them in a freight car and shipped them up to us on the farm. Those horses were a big headache and of no use to us. I remember some of them.

One horse that they sent us was an old race horse by the name of Dick. I guess he had some sort of a record. Rube, our hired man, tried him out by hitching him to the horse rake. Dick took him around the field so fast that he didn't even have time to trip the rake. He was lucky to stay on the seat. We tried using Dick as a driving horse, but he was addicted to

racing trains. If the railroad track was near the road
and a train came along Dick would bust a gut trying
to beat the train to the next crossing. Whoever was
driving him usually ended up in the ditch. My father
tried trading him off to old Lewis, but when Lewis
tried driving him he came walking home leading Dick
by the bridle, saying that he was "Too Gol Durned
much horse" for him. My father finally palmed him
off on a young blade who wanted a fast horse to show
off. Another horse that Dutton sent us was a mare by
the name of Lucille. She was a beautiful saddle horse
that had been trained to two-step to the tune of a band.
We didn't have much use for a two-stepper on the
farm. My mother's brother eventually took her over,
and for several years he and Lucille were in great
demand leading parades all over the county.

My father tried to get rid of those horses as fast
as they came in, and he became a trader of sorts. He
learned how to sell a horse without describing any of
its bad habits. We got one horse that was an outlaw.
He was a nice looking horse and was as gentle as one
could ask for until he was approached with a harness.
To him a harness meant work, and he was determined
not to have any part of it. He would tear the barn apart
before he let anyone get a harness on him. My father
got rid of him quite easily. When a buyer asked what
sort of a driving horse he was my father could honestly
answer that he did not know, because he had never
had a harness on him.

One of Dutton's shipments was meant for me.
He sent us a pony that had belonged to his daughter.
It was a shetland pony, and her entire rig came with
her. There was a russet harness and saddle, and a

A Country Life

beautifully varnished two wheeled cart. My mother liked to show off, and she would dress me up like Lord Fauntleroy and have me drive her around in the pony cart. I hated being dressed up, and I am certain that all of the other kids hated my guts whenever we showed up. The pony's name was Kit, and it soon became evident why they had shipped her to us. She had the meanest disposition of almost anything that I ever saw. She took an intense dislike to everyone on the farm except the hired man. She had a habit of unobtrusively sidling around a person she disliked and suddenly nailing him with a well aimed kick which usually hurt. One time she cornered my father in the barn and began kicking the hell out of him. If the hired man hadn't rescued him, she could have hurt him badly.

My experience with the pony once earned me a spot in a circus parade. The town of Woodsville was the mecca of our area. Besides being the shire town of the county, it was a large railroad center, and it was a place where things were happening at that time. A circus came to town every year. One year my mother took my cousin and me to see it. We went up on the train the afternoon of the day before it was due and stayed overnight with some friends. The next morning my cousin and I got up at four o'clock and went down to the freight yard to watch the circus unload and set up. There were a lot of kids there, and the boss put most of us to work, promising us a ticket to the show for our efforts. We worked like Trojans toting hay and water to the animals. When he saw that I was at home among the horses the boss began questioning me, and I told him about our horses and

my pony. He had me hitch up the circus pony and told
me that I could drive it in the parade.

The pony was small, not even half the size of
Kit, and the cart was barely big enough to have a seat
on it. The parade started about ten o'clock. The pony
and I were sandwiched in between two large animal
cages. The one in back of us was pulled by two horses
which were as large as any that I have ever seen. They
must have weighed almost a ton apiece, and their
hooves were as large as platters. After the parade
started I found out that there were things about that
pony which the circus boss had neglected to tell me.
Every few minutes the pony would stop dead in his
tracks and sit on his haunches. No matter how hard
I belabored him or yelled at him he would refuse to
move until he felt like it. I was scared to death. Those
big horses were right in back of me, and they were
towering over me and breathing down my neck. I
could hear their hooves prancing tight behind me.
About the third time the pony stopped I looked back to
see how close the horses were and saw the teamster
holding them back and laughing. I realized then that
I had a trick pony that was doing what he was trained
to do, and that I was part of his act. After that I
enjoyed the parade. That was the only time I ever
had anything to do with a circus. I can imagine that
it would have been fun to be with one for a while.

Like many people of that time, Dutton became
enamored with automobiles, and the stream of horses
from down country dried up. My uncle admitted later
that he knew the horses were of no use to us, but that
it was the best way he could find to get rid of them and
still please Mr. Dutton.

A Country Life

I think it would have been difficult to find anyone who knew more about horses and what made them tick than my Uncle George. I remember one episode in which he cured a balky horse. I had accompanied him and my grandfather to Orford where they visited a storekeeper who had been one of their boyhood friends. We rode down in my grandfather's Model T Ford. While we were at the store, a man drove up with a horse and buggy and came in and made some purchases. When he climbed in the buggy to leave, the horse refused to move. Belaboring him and swearing at him didn't make him move, and they soon began to attract an audience. Everyone was giving advice as to what to do, but the horse was stubborn and refused to abandon his balky mood.

We watched the proceedings, and after a while my uncle said that if he had a bottle of ginger soda he thought he could get the horse going. The storekeeper produced a bottle of soda that my uncle opened and poured a generous amount of it into the horse's ear. The maneuver was viewed with some skepticism by everyone including the horse, who just stood there. He didn't stand for long. In a couple of minutes he shook his head, gave a leap, and started running down the street as if the Devil was after him. The driver was bouncing around in the buggy yelling and sawing on the reins trying to stop him. They went out of sight scattering everything and everybody in their path. I don't know what happened to them, for they hadn't returned when we left for home, but I had learned of one way to get a balky horse started.

A boy growing up on a farm learned a lot about animals such as cows and horses. Some of the things

that he learned were bizarre. One of my grandfather's
sisters married a man named John, who lived in
Wentworth a short distance from the top of Atwell
hill. He was sort of a character. We visited them quite
often on Sundays. They lived quite a distance from
us, but by going through Cape Moonshine we could
approach the top of the hill in a little over two hours.
It was a long distance to drive with a horse, but my
Aunt Lizzie's Sunday dinners were worth the trip.

One Sunday we drove into the yard and John
was there beside his horse which was tied to a fence
post and was heavily hobbled. He said that he was
getting ready to worm her. Giving a horse any sort of
medicine was quite an undertaking. It usually took
two or three people to hold the horse's mouth open
and force the medicine down his throat, and I wondered how John was going to do it alone. He was
smoking the biggest pipe that I have ever seen. It was
one he had made himself out of sumac and it had a
stem which must have been way over a foot long. The
bowl was full of tobacco, and John was puffing away at
it as hard as he could. When he had a good amount of
smoke coming out of the long stem, he suddenly
rammed it up the horse's rear end, cupped both hands
around the bowl of the pipe, and blew four or five
times into it with all of the breath he could muster.
The horse must have been used to the procedure. All
that she did was to try to prance a little, but in a short
while she humped up and the damnedest bunch of
worms that one could imagine came out of her. Some
of them must have been over a foot and a half long.
When my father commented upon the procedure,
John said that the best way to worm a horse was to

A Country Life

work on the end where the worms were, rather than giving them a bunch of medicine at the other end.

All of the knowledge and tricks of the trade which we learned concerning horses became useless as the automobile rendered them obsolete. Many of the things which we consider most vital today will probably have fallen by the wayside tomorrow. That is another sure thing that can be added to death and taxes.

William S. Morse

Horseless

My first ride in an automobile occurred around 1905 when I was too young to remember it. However, it is well documented. The car was owned by one of my mother's uncles who was a doctor in Orford. It was one of the first, if not the first, automobiles in the area. I have a picture of it with Doctor Chase at the wheel and a description of the ride written by my mother. The car was a one seater without a top. It was built like a buggy, and had a dashboard which let down to make a seat at the front of the car on which my father and mother and I rode. The doctor and my aunt rode in the buggy seat. The motor must have been under the seat or under a box in back of it. My father said that the car was a Reo.

A Country Life

Sometime afterwards the doctor moved his practice to Plymouth and obtained his second car, which I remember very well. It was also a Reo. It was a large touring car with front and rear leather seats. The motor was in front under a hood. It had no top, and there were no side doors for the front seats. I always looked forward to our visits, for the doctor would take me with him when he made his rounds to visit his patients.

Doctors were the first to make practical use of the automobile in our area. In those early years of the century, they traveled the countryside making house calls on patients who were too ill to travel to their office, and they put in many long tedious hours behind old Dobbin. Although the roads were wretched for a car, they saw the automobile as a way to ease their travel time, and they made use of it whenever they could. In the early years their use of the automobile was limited to the summer months. Quite a few years elapsed before both the cars and the roads were anywhere near suitable for winter travel.

I can recall one Sunday trip that we made with the doctor. We went to Lost River, a distance of over thirty miles, which was a long and adventurous trip over the dirt roads of those days. The area between North Woodstock and Lost River was being logged. The road was worse than terrible, and we had to be pulled out of a number of holes by horses. My father knew the logging boss at Lost River, and we were invited to have dinner at camp with the lumberjacks. It was an exciting and unforgettable day.

The early automobiles were something new and different. The people who could afford them owned

86

them mainly because of their novelty, and they did not travel far from the cities or the larger towns. The cars were unreliable and subject to frequent break-downs. The rural roads were mostly a series of ruts and potholes: to venture on them was an invitation for disaster. Excursions through the countryside were made by several autos traveling together so that they could assist each other when they had trouble. They had to carry their extra fuel, and needed someone with them who knew something about cars. The farmers were skeptical of the new fangled things and had no more idea of what made them run than a goose has about God.

There is a story of an early motorist whose car conked out in front of a farmhouse on a back country road. The motorist jumped out, unbuckled the hood, and began exploring around the motor to find his trouble. After a few minutes the farmer came around and asked if he could be of any help.

"Well," the motorist said, "I guess that I need a plug, but I don't suppose that you've got such a thing."

"No, I ain't got one handy," the farmer replied, "but I can whittle one damn quick."

To a farmer those early automobiles were some-thing to pull out of a mud hole.

The old automobiles were persistent, and their numbers began to increase a little each year. Some of the horse traders began selling and trading them along with their livestock, but it was not until the end of the First World War that they became much of a factor in our area. It was around that time that my grandfather obtained an automobile in one of his trades, and our family entered the motor age.

A Country Life

The car was a Model T Ford. It was not new, but it wasn't terribly old. I would guess that it was a 1913 or 1914 model. I was in my first year of high school at that time, and my grandfather and I learned to drive it together. We had a fairly level field near the house which became our proving ground. My grandfather had quite a time learning to drive. He learned that the car was not as cooperative as a horse. Driving it was different than pulling on a pair reins and shouting at it. When we could start the car and stop it and wheel it around the field we were ready to take it on the road.

I am not sure that I could drive a Model T today. I am afraid that it would be like trying to ride a unicycle. Shifting gears was all foot work. There were three pedals on the floor under the steering column. As I recall, the pedal on the left put the car in low gear when it was pressed and held down by your foot. When you lifted your foot to release the pedal it sprang up and put the car into high gear. Low and high were the only two forward gears which the car had. Pressing down on the middle pedal, which was a little higher than the others, put the car into reverse. It was a versatile arrangement when the car was stuck in a mud hole. By pressing down on the reverse pedal and then on the low gear pedal you could rock the hell out of the car. The right hand pedal was the foot brake. The three pedals were small and close together, and until one got used to them it was easy to hit two at the same time. There was also a hand brake which had a double function. When it was pulled back and locked it was supposed to put the car in neutral.

Starting the car was like running an obstacle race. First, you had to make certain that the hand brake was pulled back and locked; otherwise the car would run over you when the motor started. Some Model T's had a tendency to advance against you even when they were in neutral. Next, the gas and spark levers had to be set. There was a quadrant on the steering wheel for the spark, and I think that the gas lever was on the steering column. They had to be set according to the idiosyncrasy of the car. After those two procedures, you were ready to go to the front of the car and try to start it by grasping the crank and spinning the motor. The crank had to be held just right, or you could end up with a broken wrist if the motor kicked back. The choke was set by a ring attached to a wire which had to be pulled by the left hand while the motor was being cranked. If everything went well and the motor started, you had to drop the crank as if it was a hot potato and run like hell back to the steering wheel and fiddle with the spark and the gas levers to keep the motor running. The motor could be cantankerous and refuse to start no matter how hard and fast you cranked it, especially when the weather was cold. Sometimes a rear wheel had to be jacked up so that it would turn freely which made it easier to spin the motor.

It was of no concern at that time, but anyone riding in the front seat of those old Model T's was sitting on top of the gas tank. In order to fill up with gas everyone had to get out of the front seat so that the cushion could be removed to gain access to the filler cap. After the tank was filled and the cushion replaced, one had to go through the cranking process all over again before taking off. There was no gas gauge. If the gas in the tank became low enough, the motor would

A Country Life

conk out when going up a hill. The usual procedure in such a case was to coast backwards down the hill, turn the car around and climb the hill by backing up it in reverse gear. Many people carried an extra can of gas in the car as well.

The old Model T was the jeep of its time. The other cars were ponderous and heavy. They had a touch of luxury, as they were mostly the playthings of the rich and well to do. The Ford was light with no frills, and it had a high clearance. Its suspension was such that the wheels and axles seemed to float, and they adjusted to uneven ground by racking and twisting themselves like a shimmy dancer. It was ideally suited to the rough and rutty roads of those days, and could travel in places where the larger cars feared to tread. Also, it was cheaper than the other cars, and a little haywire and a hammer could remedy many of its troubles.

When the farmers and other people of the rural areas recognized the Ford's versatility they took to it like a duck takes to water. A farmer could remove the rear seat cushion, load a half dozen forty quart cans of milk in the car, travel two or three miles or more to the creamery, and be back home in jig time. The same trip with old Dobbin spoiled a large part of the forenoon. On Sundays he and the family could travel fifteen or twenty miles, spend the day visiting friends or relatives, and return home in plenty of time to do the evening milking. Saturday nights he could load his wife and kids into the car, travel to some of the larger towns, shop a bit, see the sights, and do a little carousing. It was truly a liberation from the isolated and humdrum existence of the farm. The tempo of

William S. Morse

life began to move a little bit faster.

As automobiles increased in number people began to clamor for better roads. The main roads that connected the villages and larger towns were improved by surfacing them with gravel, but the rural roads leading to the foothills and the back farms did not receive much of any treatment. For many years traveling over them with a car in the spring and winter months was a daunting procedure. Many people jacked their cars up and stored them in the carriage shed, and old Dobbin still ruled the roads for a large part of the time. When they first started plowing the rural roads in the winter they made a bad situation worse. The plows exposed enough bare ground so that sledding was difficult, and they left so much snow and ice in the roads that a car spent more time getting out of trouble than it did traveling.

Eventually the autos and the plows won out, and old Dobbin's days were numbered. Now things have reversed themselves. Today automobiles belong to the masses, and Dobbin is a plaything of the rich and well to do.

Visitors

Back in the early years of the century rural areas such as ours that were quite a long distance from the cities were known as the boondocks. Those who "lived in the sticks" were generally considered to be country bumpkins living a dull and monotonous life. Even our relatives who lived in the cities tended to be somewhat disparaging unless they wanted something from us.

We had relatives in profusion. Everyone who had any connection whatsoever with my father's or mother's family was known as an Aunt, Uncle, or Cousin. With the exception of a cousin who had a farm near us, my father's relatives were sisters and aunts, and they all lived in cities. One of his aunts

William S. Morse

lived in New York, and the rest of his relatives lived in or around Boston. My mother had two aunts who lived within thirty miles of us, but she also had distant relatives who lived in Michigan. It didn't make any difference how far away they lived, or how far-fetched their relationship was to us, or if they considered us as living in the sticks, the farm was a mecca for them every summer. It was a place for them to visit and to spend their vacations.

A visit by relatives in those days was not a whirlwind tour or a week-end sojourn: their descent upon us could last one or two weeks. They made their invasion by train, and they did not travel light. They came to stay for "a while," and they had trunks. When they arrived a trunk full of clothes came with them. If they had children there would probably be two trunks. When we drove down to the depot to meet them, the hired man sometimes had to come along with a wagon to take care of the baggage. During the summer months the house would often be overflowing with relatives and their trunks. Some of those trunks were large. They were built to take a banging, and a lot of them have survived. They are in demand today, for antique dealers refurbish them and sell them for a lot of money. I don't know what people do with them, but in those days finding a place to put them where they would not be in the way was a problem.

We were not the only ones who had company. Our neighbor, who had a small farm only a short distance across the road, had a daughter with three children. Every year they came visiting and stayed for the entire summer, so we were not lonesome. Our house was a crowded and busy place, and there were

A Country Life

times when you had to wait for your turn to use the privy.

Our visiting season started early in the summer. My father had an Aunt Edna who was a widow. She had married one of his uncles who was a Civil War veteran, and he was buried in our district cemetery. She would come and stay a week for Memorial Day. When I was old enough I would meet her at the depot and the station agent would help me wrestle her trunk aboard the buggy. She didn't seem to have any assortment of clothes in it for she always wore a black dress. She resembled a buxom Whistler's Mother.

Every afternoon if it didn't rain someone would have to drive her to the cemetery where she would fuss around Sime's grave and plant flowers. He must have had the most decorated grave in the county. Memorial Day was an important event. Many of the Civil War veterans were living, and it was their day to bask in the sun. It was a time of solemnity with large parades, and many ceremonies. There were lengthy orations by politicians, and every veteran had a chance to speak his piece and relive his war time experiences. Many were long-winded and they took up the entire day. A lot of the kids were roped in to participate. Every Memorial Day when I was a young boy I had to stand and face a bunch of people and recite a piece about a bugle boy. Aunt Edna participated in the ceremonies, and her visit ended a day or so afterwards. We would load her and her trunk on the train and watch her depart for her home down country.

June and July seemed to be the months for my father's sisters and aunts to visit. They had children, and I had someone to play and fight with. I learned some of their city ways and they became acquainted with our country life. Perhaps it was beneficial to us, but I was usually glad to see them depart for home.

My mother's relatives from Michigan kept the house full during the month of August. There were several of them, and they took turns with their visits. They were participating in the rapid growth of the auto industry and by our standards they were quite affluent. When the roads were improved, they traveled by car, and they didn't have any trunks to lift and push around. They were antique hounds, and we enjoyed traveling the countryside with them. They usually had the latest model automobiles, and we looked forward to their visits and to riding in the big leather upholstered cars of those early days. Many of those old automobiles could offer some of our modern cars a point or two about luxury and comfort. The seats were large and quite high; a person could see around the countryside and one had room to spread out. Each one was distinctive, and they had a smell that was a mixture of old leather and gasoline which was quite pleasing.

Those summer visitors did not contribute any help towards the work on the farm. Their presence was sometimes disruptive to it, and my father would refer to them as deadheads. We rarely went to the city to visit them, for we saw enough of them during the summer. My father often told me that I would avoid a lot of trouble if I stayed away from my relatives, and I guess that there were times when he became tired of having them around.

95

Mountain Years

For three summers of my boyhood my parents lived on a mountain top. Our recollections of the places and events of the early years of our life are often enhanced and exaggerated with the passage of time, but my memories of those three years need no enhancement. The mountain was Mount Moosilauke, the dominant peak of the third highest range of mountains in New Hampshire. Living there was a privilege which has been bestowed upon but few people. To a boy on the threshold of his teens, living on top of the 4800 foot peak was like dwelling in the abode of the Gods on Olympus.

In the fall of 1914 my father became seriously ill with pneumonia, and when he recovered he was unable to continue with the hard work of farming and logging which he had been doing. My parents were not accustomed to being idle for long, and they took up the task of running the hotel that was perched on the highest point of the mountain. The oldest part of the hotel was built of stone, and, although it had nothing to do with my parents running it, it is interesting to note that it was built by my great grandfather, Darius Swain, in partnership with James Clement, in the year 1860.

Agreeing to the management of the hotel was a pig in a poke sort of thing. Neither my father or my mother had visited the top of the mountain to inspect the place at close quarters. Their only acquaintance with it was the distant views which they had seen from the river valley, which was miles away. The hotel was aptly named the Tip Top House, and from the start my parents had some misgivings about agreeing to run it. Their doubts increased when we made our first ascent of the mountain early in May in 1915.

Our route was by the carriage road which ran from the foot of the mountain in Warren to the top which is in the town of Benton. The road was built in 1870 for the purpose of transporting passengers and supplies up the mountain, and in our day it was showing its age. It was traveled by a stage composed of a pair of horses pulling a conveyance of ancient usage, which was called a buckboard: a vehicle with four wheels attached to a platform of springy boards. It was conceived for rough traveling, and can best be described as a trampoline with a couple of buggy seats that was mounted on wheels. Samuel Drake, who rode up the mountain around 1882, described it as one of the most ill-favored things he had ever seen, and wrote at that time that the road was no bed of roses. I never traveled on the rig, but guests who rode it up the mountain often complained of the jolting which they received. If it traveled with any sort of speed when it descended the mountain, the ones riding in it must have resembled dice being shaken in a chuckaluck cage. Early accounts indicate that it was once a popular way of reaching the top, but in our day most people hiked the trails. The stage was used to tote supplies and elderly guests up the mountain. There were three other trails, each of which was much shorter than the road. We had picked the longest route to the top.

The stage accompanied us on our first trip up the mountain, carrying supplies. We walked, and I remember that ascent very well, for we began to think that we would never reach the top. It was supposed to be five miles from the toll gate to the top of the mountain, but few ever walked it who thought it was less than eight. From time to time we would get a glimpse of the top and the house, and each time that we did so it did not appear to be any closer than it had an hour before. When we finally reached the end of timberline on the ridge, the house, perched on the peak of the bald cone, still seemed to be a long way off. Fortunately, it was a nice day. If the mountain had presented us with one of its violent moods we would have undoubtedly abandoned the project.

Their first inspection of the house was also discouraging to my parents. The house had not been open for several years, and it required a lot of work to make it suitable for guests. We had three men with us who had been hired for that purpose, and in two or

William S. Morse

three weeks time we were open for business.

That was an era in which the White Mountain hotels were flourishing. They were large, luxurious places built to accommodate hundreds of guests, who would arrive by train and stage with baggage enough for an extended stay. Compared to them, the Tip Top House was not much more than a hostel which offered food and lodging. However, it was on a mountain top that provided a sweeping view of five states and Canada. To the people who made an extended stay it offered a chance to experience the many moods of the mountain. Those moods ranged from days on the mountain top that were sunny and benign, to being enveloped for days at a time by clouds that were swept across the peak by violent winds – winds that were strong enough to have blown the house away if it had not been anchored to the mountain top by thick iron rods. The mountain also offered a chance for solitude, which was something cherished by some people. Many took the opportunity to experience it by staying for a week or so, and there were a few who made a longer stay of a month or more.

The house was not at all luxurious, but my parents made it homey and comfortable, and the meals that my mother served quickly gave it a reputation for excellence. The rooms were not much more than cubicles with austere furnishings: a wash bowl and pitcher on a stand and a thundermug under the bed. The house could take care of forty to fifty people quite easily, and in spite of its rough accommodations it was often filled to capacity. Mountain hiking was popular at that time, and Moosilauke with its Tip Top House was a magnet.

A Country Life

There were times, when we had a lot of people to feed and accommodate, that I had to help out by washing and drying dishes and assisting as clerk in the office. I learned something about running a hotel and catering to people, but most of the time I was footloose. I had a dog that was always with me, and we had the run of the mountain. We explored its nooks and crannies, and learned of its pitfalls and its scenic attractions.

There was an old register at the house that had been made into a scrap book. It had clippings that told of frequent ascents of the mountain, and described its unspoiled attractions to which trails had been established. In the later years of the 1800's people evidently traveled those trails and visited the spots to which they led, lured to them by extensive publicity which was put out by the Boston and Maine railroad. At the time we went on the mountain the custom of visiting them had ceased. The old trails had become obliterated, and the wild scenic spots at which they terminated were mostly unknown.

The accounts were intriguing. With my dog I searched for those trails and reopened them, ending up in what seemed to me at that time to be some of the wildest places imaginable. The effort was rewarding, for I guided many of our guests to the most scenic and wildest spots. I also discovered some productive fishing holes that many guests were anxious to try. I learned that a good catch of fish could result in a liberal tip.

Moosilauke is wild. The headwaters of the Baker River, the Wild Ammonoosuc and the Oliverian originate high on the mountain. They are

William S. Morse

spectacular, cascading over precipitous gorges and through deep ravines. However, they are high on the mountain away from the main trails, and even at the present time I suspect that they are not visited by the run of the mill hikers. Searching them out and exploring them was an adventure in which I acquired a great amount of mountain lore and a knowledge of the woods that resulted in a lifelong association with them.

During the period that we were on the mountain we experienced many storms. Some of them were awesome. There were times when we would be in clouds for several days without seeing the world below. The storms were usually accompanied by winds, but there were rare occasions when the clouds settled quietly upon us in a gray and wraith-like silence. The storms came from all quarters of the compass. To the west we could see what the weather was like as far away as the Adirondacks, and we could observe it traveling our way across the Green Mountains and the Connecticut Valley. As I recall, our most severe storms seemed to come from the east. From our high point on top of the mountain we could watch them building up on the southeastern horizon, which is the Atlantic Ocean, and observe them approaching over the intervening land mass – sometimes with amazing speed. The storms hit us with severe winds which would drive the clouds racing across the mountain top and rattle the rods that held the house down.

Those rods must have been at least an inch thick, and were anchored by means of eye bolts sunk in the ledges which formed the mountain top. The rods were spliced by eyes in their ends which created quite a bit of slack in them, and when the wind was severe it would literally pick the house up until the slack was taken up. The rods would then rudely jerk the house back to earth with a jar. Trying to get some sleep at night when the house was moving up and down with the wind was difficult. Guests who were riding out a storm and had never experienced such a thing often became greatly alarmed.

Storm clouds were dark and foreboding, and we often had to have lamps burning most of the day when we were in them. Visibility outside could be limited to fifty feet or less, and hikers encountering such storms could often get lost and have a panicky experience before finding the house. My father had a forty-five caliber revolver which he used to fire late in the afternoon on stormy days to guide those who might be disoriented, and there were several times when I accompanied him traveling the mountain looking for people who were lost.

Thunderstorms almost always occurred far below us, and it was awe inspiring to look down upon their clouds and see the lightning playing around them. They, and the fires which they caused, could be seen for some distance around the countryside. The places which the lightning hit were probably barns, as subsistence farms predominated in the area at that time. Experiencing the storms which occurred instilled a healthy respect for nature and its elements in all of us.

Sunrises and sunsets were strong attractions to those who were enamored of the mountain. Many people came up the mountain for the express purpose of observing them. It was one of my chores to arouse those who wished to see the sun rise, and I had to get up around four o'clock to do so. At the top of the 4800 foot peak both events occur when the world below is in partial darkness. There is no description that can do justice to them. As the sun's rim first peeks over the White Mountains which form the eastern horizon, and as it finally ducks behind the Adirondacks which are on the western horizon, it rises and sets with a rapidity which makes one realize how fast the world on which we live is spinning. Both events are spectacular and colorful. It is difficult to believe that anyone could observe either of them without experiencing a deep and humble sense of reverence. They are the most impressive memories of my experiences on the mountain.

Around the end of September we would board up all of the openings in the house for the winter and return to the farm. My father had kept just enough of the farm going to keep the hired man occupied, and with the exception of the hunting season and sugaring, our winter months were not very busy or exciting. We would return to the mountain around the first of May and reopen the house for another season. The mountain was not visited in the winter in those days, and we would find the house pretty much as we had left it the previous fall.

We were on the mountain top until the end of the 1917 season. My father tried to purchase the property, but the majority shareholders became owners and they gave it to Dartmouth College. To the best of my knowledge, my parents were the last ones to run the house as a hotel.

A Country Life

The house is now gone. It was destroyed in 1942 by fire which was probably caused by lightning. The fact that it withstood the elements for many years is a tribute to the staunchness of its construction. To me the peak is now strangely bare, and I am thankful that for three years I was fortunate enough to be able to call it home.

William S. Morse

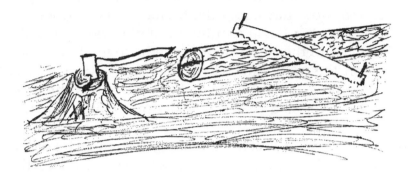

Logs

"Git up there in the collar, you S-O-B's. You can't pull logs layin' back here in the breechin'." Those were the words of a burly, redheaded teamster urging his horses to a greater effort, and they are my first recollection of a logging job. I was young, probably not much more than seven years old at the time, which would have been around 1911. I had accompanied my father to a logging operation that he had going and where he had a number of men working. He had to travel to some other part of the job, and he left me in the care of the teamster telling him to look after me. The teamster did so by putting me on the back of one of his horses and shoving me forward on its withers where I could hang onto the hames while he continued with his work of yarding logs.

A Country Life

The fall and winter months were the logging
season in those days, and the hauling was all done by
horses. During those months my father delegated the
farm work to the hired man while he logged. He had a
camp on the mountain where he employed men to cut
logs that were loaded on bob sleds and hauled by teams
of horses over sled roads to a saw mill which was three
or four miles away. His operation was known as a
two sled job, and when we were about ten years old a
cousin and I haunted the camp whenever we had time
off from school. We traveled with the teams and were
often put to work as road monkeys shoveling snow
and spreading hay and sand as they were needed to
brake the loads on the hills. The lumberjacks were
partial to us, granting us the privilege of running
errands for them, and they showed us some of the
tricks of their trade. They taught us how to pull a
crosscut saw without leaning on it. We learned how to
throw a hitch on a log, and we picked up the jargon of
the woods. When they talked of putting a vandyke on
a log or of using a snub warp we knew what they were
talking about. We also learned to swear, an attainment
which sorely vexed our mothers.

In the fall of 1914 my father was seriously ill
with pneumonia. When he recovered, he was not able
to work as he had been doing. He had to discontinue
logging, and it was about sixteen years later before I
became reacquainted with the woods and the industry.
By that time the heyday of the large timber operations
when logs were transported to the mills by railroads
built into the heavily timbered areas, was over. The
long log drives down the Connecticut river, which I
remember watching when I was a boy, had ceased. The

tales of the riotous river drivers and the bivouacs of Old Colorado in which she entertained them were legends. There were few areas of any size left for the independent operators to cut. The areas which had been ravished by the timber barons had been taken over by the National Forest and the State, and the paper companies owned a large share of the timber which was left.

About 1929 I began practicing as a land surveyor. A large percentage of my work involved the surveying of wild lands for various lumber and timber operators. In the early 1930's I began surveying for Paul Glover, one of the large operators of the area. With the exception of two years with the Forest Service salvaging timber that was laid low by the 1938 hurricane, I worked with him until 1955. We logged our way from Indian and Perry Streams in northern New Hampshire through central New Hampshire and Vermont to the Adirondacks, where we ended up cutting a large tract of International Paper Company land. It was a good relationship. Paul handled the front end – the contracts with the mills and the paper companies, the financing, legal matters, etc. – and I handled the woods operations.

We always had a number of jobs going, ranging from small ones with camps of fifteen or twenty men to larger camps of fifty or sixty men. We cut both pulpwood and logs. Our heaviest cut was pulpwood, which was sold to the paper mills. Our log cut was mostly hardwood which went to the furniture companies. Our usual procedure was to set a sawmill on or near the job, saw the logs and deliver the lumber to them by sticking it at the nearest railroad siding. We also cut and sold railroad ties, maple bolts for heel stock, and logs for veneer mills.

In the early nineteen thirties logging was done by following the old time-honored procedures. Trees were felled and logs were cut by men using axes and crosscut saws. Logs were twitched out to a yard by horses, and from there they were two sledded to the mill, which usually had to be done on snow. The paper mills would accept only peeled pulpwood in those days. It was cut and peeled during the summer months and yarded out during the winter. The wood was then hauled to the nearest railroad siding where it was loaded in box cars and shipped to the paper mills.

The logging was done by men who were experienced and adept at using the tools of their trade. They could make chips fly with an axe, and they could file a saw so that it would go through timber as if it were butter. Teamsters knew how to handle horses. They knew what horses could do and how to make them do it, and they knew how to take care of them. It was all an operation as old as the hills, but it was on the threshold of several changes which would eventually take the fun out of logging.

The first change occurred in transportation with the appearance of trucks, which were pretty well in evidence by 1930. They were a far cry from the heavy rigs used today, but they were effective in hauling logs to the mills and pulpwood to the rail sidings. Throughout the nineteen forties they progressed to the stage where they could bypass many of the sidings and haul pay loads for a distance of over one hundred miles directly to the mills. Crawler tractors and bull-dozers also made their appearance, and horses and teamsters began to disappear. Tractors could haul logs and pulpwood to the yards regardless of the season of the year, and bulldozers could build summer and winter truck roads long distances through the woods to the loading yards. On our last job in the Adirondacks we built about ten miles of gravel roads that were much better than a lot of the town roads, and we must have built twenty five miles or more of winter truck roads.

The mechanization of the lumberjack took some time and persistence. In the later half of the nineteen forties we were in Vermont making a cut of twenty to twenty five thousand cords of pulpwood a year which went to International Paper. They were interested in making pulpwood operations more efficient, and they began sending us power saws to experiment with. The first saw that they sent us was a monstrosity. It was a duplicate of a crosscut saw with a blade at least five feet in length which had a saw chain around it. It had a heavy motor on one end, and it took a man at each end to run it. It took two men to carry the damn thing, and it quickly became an object of ridicule.

Another saw that they sent us was a circular saw about twenty inches in diameter that was mounted between two bicycle wheels so that it could be wheeled through the woods. The saw was mounted at the end of a long handle that was swiveled so that it could be used to cut vertically or horizontally. Whoever put it together probably had a vision of wheeling it up to a tree and sawing it down and then turning the blade over and sawing the tree into pulpwood lengths. It might have worked in a park, but it was of no use in the rock bound hills of Vermont. We tried using it to saw pulpwood in the yard, but found out that it was a lethal thing. If the saw inadvertently hit the ground while it was running, it would gallop away through the woods at a terrific speed, gyrating wildly until it destructed itself by hitting trees or stones.

Another saw that we experimented with was an electric chain saw. It received its power by means of a long cord which ran from a gas driven generator set at the foot of the strip. The tangle created by the cord and the brush as the cut moved up the strip generated nothing but curses and frustration, and that idea was quickly abandoned.

The saws gradually improved, but for some time they were of questionable value. They were continually subject to mechanical breakdowns, and a good man with a bucksaw could out produce them. Eventually, around 1948 or 1949, the chain saw began to evolve into its present form and the axe and the crosscut saws and bucksaws disappeared. The lumber-jack had to learn to become adept at falling trees with a chain saw instead of notching them with an axe, and he also had to become a mechanic. Logging had become fully mechanized. I have not been on a logging job since 1956, and I imagine that much more mechanization has taken place since that time.

To me one big difference between the logging operations of the earlier years – the pre World War II days – and the later days of mechanization was in the noise level. In the old days a logging operation was relatively quiet. The silence of the woods was broken only by the curses of the teamsters as they urged their horses into their collars; the echo of the axes as they bit their way into timber; the swish of the crosscut saws as they were pulled through wood; and the crash of a tree as it fell. Those were the sounds which a man listened for as he walked a job. By them he determined the number of crews that were working and their degree of productivity.

At the time I stopped logging in the Adirondacks the operation was fully mechanized. Although I rarely used tractors as I felt that horses were more dependable and less destructive, the cutting was all done by chain saws – sometimes from one hundred and fifty man camps. We had bulldozers building roads and log loaders and pulpwood loaders loading trucks. They were all raucous and noisome, and compared to the old days the woods sounded like a boiler factory. One did not have to listen; the clamor made by the machines was forced upon him.

Snow and Neally Company of Bangor was the big provider of logging supplies in the Northeast. For years they guaranteed all of their axes. If an axe broke or chipped on the job, they would replace it with a new one. Shortly after we moved into the Adirondacks they issued a circular in which they withdrew their guarantee, stating that there were no axemen left who knew how to use an axe or to properly take care of one. To me that withdrawal spoke volumes of the changes which had taken place. The only thing that had escaped mechanization was the cook shack.

Jacks

The Reverend Timothy Dwight,
who traveled extensively in New England in the
late years of the 1700's and the first decade of the 1800's,
viewed the lumber industry with a jaundiced eye. He
called it a dissolute business, and described those who
were engaged in it as ..."haunters of taverns, prone to
profaneness, prodigality, immoderate drinking and
other ruinous habits." If he had been on the scene one
hundred and fifty years later, he would probably have
made the same observation, and he might have added
some other traits to his description. Throughout
the years since his time, writers and observers of the
industry have pretty well established loggers as a breed
of men who were at times Holy Terrors.

William S. Morse

The legends of the men of the West and their lives have been given glamour and enhanced by stressing their commitment to the use of the six gun to commit mayhem. The loggers were here before they were, and they were tough enough to disdain the use of anything but spiked boots to accomplish their ends. They did not ride horses over the countryside – they rode logs down the river.

In New England the early settlers were the ones who first tackled the forest. It was at their doorstep and had to be removed to let daylight in for their crops. They were primarily farmers. It seems that they burned or girdled many of the trees to get rid of them, but the pine was a lordly and useful tree. Those that were not used for masts could be made into lumber and utilized for building or for export. It was from such trees that the first logs were probably cut, and sawmills made an early appearance.

By the time Timothy Dwight made his travels, the process had been going on for one hundred and fifty years. The southern parts of New England were fairly well settled by that time. It is likely that the pine which was readily accessible had been cut, and it had become necessary to reach back up the rivers and into what was then the back country for the timber which was in demand. Logging camps and the men who inhabited them began to make their appearance. It was pine that they were after. Spruce was considered to be of such little value that Ira Allen gloated about deceitfully unloading a Vermont township of it onto some unwary speculators.

The pines were ages old, and they were huge. There are reports of trees five and six feet through,

breast high, and of stumps large enough to allow
standing room for a pair of oxen. John Springer, who
logged in Maine in the early 1800's, wrote of cutting
a pine that topped off at 144 feet. It made five logs
which loaded a six ox team three times, and it took
him around two hours to chop it down. The butt log
was so large that the stream did not have water
enough to float it and it had to be left behind.

Those trees were cut by men with axes. After
a season of toppling such giants and then riding
them down the river to their destination, the loggers
undoubtedly felt that they had earned some relaxation
and entertainment, and in the course of obtaining
them they must have enlivened what had previously
been staid towns. Some of their frolics could have
been as awesome as the trees they had cut, and they
probably led to Timothy Dwight's observation. The
loggers' reputation for carousal has followed them
down through the years.

I first became acquainted with loggers when I
was a kid around the end of the first decade of the
century. My father had a farm, but in the winter
months he used to take on logging jobs, cutting and
delivering logs to the mill. There was a camp on the
mountain which accommodated the men, and when I
was around ten years old I used to hang out around it.
Most of the teamsters were local farmers who wanted
winter's work for their horses, but the falling and
yarding was done by dyed in the wool loggers. Two
of them that I remember were considered to be old
timers. One had white hair and a heavy flowing white
beard that earned him the name of Santa Claus. He
was tough. He never bundled up in the severest cold

weather, and all that he wore on his feet were rubber boots, disdaining even the use of stockings, which must have been about the same as being barefoot. The other old timer was a swamper by the name of Joe Christmas. I think that his original name was Joe Noel, but over the years it had been bastardized to Joe Christmas, and that became his handle. He was not as old as Santa, but in listening to their talk of the different jobs and log drives that they had worked on in years past, it became evident that he had been around for a while. They had both, as my father described them, "seen the elephant."

It was the early nineteen thirties before I became actively engaged in woods operations. By that time real old timers like Santa and Joe were gone. However, the operations of the large paper companies and a few lumber companies had nurtured a breed of men who were at home in the woods. I do not know when the term lumberjack was coined or the circumstances of its creation – it may have originally been meant to be a word of opprobrium – but it was seldom used either by the men themselves or by those who employed them. They were loggers. When we ordered men for the woods from those who serviced the industry, we ordered according to our needs. There were axemen, teamsters, fallers, yardmen and sled tenders, swampers, stablemen, pulpwood cutters, blacksmiths, wood butchers, cooks and cookies, bull cooks, tong men, etc. There were many specialties, and the ones who performed them were all known as loggers.

The majority of the men who worked in the woods were of French Canadian descent, but there were many men of many nationalities. There were Russians, Poles, Finns, Swedes and Norwegians, and a few Indians and Negroes who answered the call. Cutting logs and pulpwood seemed to be the only work which they performed, and for many of them the woods and the bunkhouse were the only home which they knew.

A man in a logging camp that is back in the woods is pretty well out of circulation, and many of them preferred it that way. They might be on the dodge from a family, from alimony payments or creditors, or even from the law itself. An isolated logging camp was an ideal place to take cover. The food was the best. The bunks were nothing to write home about – they were often "muzzle loaders" which had to be entered from the foot – but the bunk house was kept clean by the bull cook. The atmosphere could be aromatic at times, smelling of unwashed bodies, of wet clothes hanging over the hot stove to dry, and of rum farts when a new shipment of men came in, but taken all in all it was not too bad a place to hide out. We were often queried by the law men about some of the men in our camps, and there was a time during the depression when they overwhelmed us.

During those years Canada was as hard up for jobs as we in this country were. One year we had a large jobber from Lewiston cutting Smart's mountain, and we also had camps in the area between Smart's and Canaan, including Holt's Ledge area. A large number of the men shipping out of Lewiston were line jumpers who had entered this country illegally to work in the woods, and the Immigration Service raided our camps periodically. They would show up in

William S. Morse

force, surrounding a camp at midnight, and often take one half of the men out with them to return them to Canada. In a week's time most of the same men would be back cutting wood on the same strip.

The pay during those years was too small to allow for much riotous living, but there were characters who stirred things up at times. One such character was a man known by the name of Bucksaw Sam who worked for us in Vermont. He was an Indian who claimed that he came from Oldtown. The name followed his reputation as being a ten cord man, which meant that at some time in the past he had performed the feat of sawing and piling ten cords of pulpwood on a yard in one day. That was in the era BC (before chain saws), when wood was sawed by a man pulling a bucksaw, and chunking up a daily production of ten cords in such a manner is not an insignificant accomplishment.

Sam was good for a stint of eight or ten weeks in the woods before he began to yearn to view something besides trees and a horse's rear end. He would tidy up his yard, hang up his saw, and hit the tote road to headquarters where he would draw some money and proceed with his plans. The head clerk would let us know that he was loose, and after four or five days we began anticipating a phone call. It seems that when Sam's intake of liquor reached a certain stage he would begin to brood over the injustices which his race had suffered from the white man. He must have had a few bar room brawls, but he would usually end up going on the warpath, war whooping down the streets of town, brandishing the nearest thing he could find that resembled a tomahawk. He never harmed anyone or caused much damage, and the police never complained of unusual trouble rounding him up. I would pay his fine and damages and send someone to pick him up and return him to camp.

It is a strange analogy, but there seemed to be some correlation between a man and the drunk he indulged in. The better the man the bigger his drunk. Our volume production was pulpwood, and in the prewar years the mills would accept only peeled wood. Peeling season was short. Wood started peeling around the end of April and tightened up soon after Labor Day, so we only had four months to make our contract. A good man would produce from one hundred to one hundred and fifty cords during the season, and there was a big demand for them.

Top dog in those years was a man who could rightly boast of being a two hundred cord man. I shall call him Auguste, as it may be best not to use his real name. It should be pointed out that the wood was cut and peeled in those days by a man using an axe, a spud, and a bucksaw. Auguste would only drop and peel his strip during the peeling season, waiting until after Labor Day to saw it up. He was a daylight to dark man, and he made every move count. Each Fourth of July he would draw some money, saying that he needed a few days of rest. I never saw him when he was resting, but the men said that he did so by getting drunk as fast as he could and by staying that way. Some of his exploits were the talk of the bunk house. He was certainly the worst for wear when he returned to the job, but he would shape up and go back to peeling wood. One Fourth of July he returned to camp with a monkey that he had picked up while he rested. That monkey became the scourge of the camp, and the turnover of cooks was high. If it had been anyone but Auguste, he would have been run out of camp.

By Fair time wood had stopped peeling – the pressure was off, and the men were ready for a blow out. They disrupted and enlivened many a midway. They would have their pulpwood sawed and piled by the end of October. The scale would be in, and we would know how close we were to our contract, and whether we were going to make or lose on it. Whichever way it came out, we would be busy starting the fall and winter logging jobs, which would mean another hectic four or five months. It was like having a tiger by the tail.

Bender

The city of Brooklyn is the most unlikely place where one would look for lumberjacks. For a period of three or four years, while we were operating in Vermont, a Finn who went by the name of Fred Bender would show up around the first of April looking for a pulpwood job. He wanted a small job of twelve to fifteen hundred cords to peel and pile at the stump. Most of the jobbers at that time wanted to peel and deliver the wood to a truck road so that they would have a winter's job for their men and horses yarding the wood, but Fred didn't like Vermont winters. He didn't like horses either. He came from Brooklyn, and when he found a job that suited him and had signed the contract to peel it, he would head back home.

William S. Morse

In about a week's time he would show up at headquarters with four or five taxi loads of men – all Finns, and all of them from Brooklyn. Moreover, and what was most unusual, they would all be sober. They would head into the woods, put up a camp, and be ready to start cutting as soon as wood started to peel. Fred ran a camp that was as trouble free and efficient as one could ask for. His camp was small with a bunk house and cook room under one roof, and a one horse hovel and a sauna beside it. If his men had any carousels, they were confined to camp, and we never knew of them. Some Saturdays a couple of them would show up at headquarters to draw a little money so that they could go to "Rootland" and shop. At that time a man named Mike had a beer joint on Wales street with a flop house across the street from it which was a rendezvous for lumberjacks. I used to send someone with a car to his place Monday mornings, and we could usually pick up a load or two of good men. Fred's two Finns would be waiting for us, and I think that they really did shop for the rest of their camp for they always had quite a few bundles with them.

Bender's entire camp dropped and peeled all summer, and did not start sawing up and piling until after Labor Day. They were proud of their work and did the best job of stump cutting that I have ever seen. Their wood was closely knotted and carefully piled, and their strips were so cleanly swamped that the wood could be yarded on six inches of snow. There were men of other nationalities who produced more wood, but those Finns were not far behind, and they did a much cleaner and better job. When the job was

A Country Life

piled and scaled, Fred and his men would come tramping into headquarters to settle up. Fred, and also many of his men, would not draw a cent all summer, and the few that had drawn money had done so sparingly. Every year when that camp settled up it was one hell of a hit, amounting to several thousand dollars, and they would think that it was a huge joke. They all headed back to Brooklyn with the money, and I suppose that they holed up there for the winter. Fred and his men cut for us several summers, but in 1949 and 1950 we began to run out of wood in Vermont, and they did not follow us to the Adirondacks.

If all of the jobs had gone as smoothly as Bender's our life would have been a bed of roses, but it was a rare exception. Most of the jobs were larger, which accounted for a lot of the problems, but it was hard to find a jobber who could keep his men producing all season. We had a Russian who was good for three or four thousand cords of wood a year, which was produced in the intervals between mighty orgies. His camp was ethnic in its make up, as he attracted Russians, Poles and other Slavs who flocked to him. They would cut wood to beat hell for several weeks before they drew any money, and then the camp would explode. Charlie, the jobber, was as bad as any of his men. One morning, when he was drunk, he got mad at the cook and went for him with a butcher knife shouting, "Me kill!" The cook, whose name was Hebert, had a huge skillet on the stove in which he had a mess of eggs and bacon frying in sizzling hot fat. "Not me!" he said, and he upended the skillet, hot eggs, bacon and fat over Charlie's head. It tamed him down and burned him so badly that he had to go to the hospital. Hebert walked out, and we had to find a new cook for Charlie.

Many of the camps which we had were ethnic in character, and unlike Bender and his Finns they were troublesome at times. During the war there was a shortage of good woodsmen, and we ran almost one hundred percent Canadians. We had one jobber who went far up into Quebec, and came back with a bunch of Indians. They were good men, and they piled up a lot of pulpwood before they drew any money. When they did, their rampage bordered onto mayhem. We had to send them back to Canada, and from then on we kept a sharp eye on the crews that our jobbers used. Men of French Canadian descent produced most of our logs and pulpwood, and were the least troublesome. When they sought surcease from their labors they did so away from camp, and production in a French Canadian camp was seldom disrupted.

Some of the jobbers could take you over the coals if you were not careful. We purchased a large tract of spruce from an estate. The land was all in Reading and Cavendish except for a tag end which was an abandoned farm in Topsham about seventy miles from our operation. I didn't want to bother with it, but we owned it and decided to try to cut it. It was a poor job, with only about five or six hundred cords of poor quality spruce scattered over it. It had a house and a barn on it which could serve as a camp, and there was a good sugar house which was well equipped. A good sugar orchard was about the only thing of much value on the place. I anticipated a lot of trouble finding someone to cut it, but much to my surprise a small jobber whose first name was Pierre jumped at the job.

A Country Life

He had cut for us before. He liked a small job where he could use five or six men in a small camp, and his wife could cook for the outfit. The job was so far away that I didn't pay much attention to it. Everytime I went on the job Pierre had produced a little pulpwood, but the wood was so poor that no one would cut it by the cord. He was paying the men day wages to cut it, and it was getting to be expensive wood.

Around the middle of April one of the men called headquarters informing them that Pierre had pulled out, and that I had better come up. When I arrived I found out what had probably been in Pierre's mind when he first agreed to cut the job. He had taken the men, who were on our payroll, and put them to work tapping maples and hauling sap while he fired up the evaporator and made syrup. The men said that he made about three hundred gallons of syrup. He loaded it and his wife into a rented truck and pulled out. We never saw him again. He had made off with around twenty five hundred dollars worth of syrup which we had paid to produce, and left us with a few hundred cords of measly pulpwood which had cost enough money to be covered with diamonds.

William S. Morse

The 18th

On January 14, 1919, the State of Nebraska added to its distinction by becoming the thirty-sixth state to ratify the Eighteenth Amendment, thus making the manufacture, sale, or transportation of intoxicating liquors for beverage purposes a crime. The amendment did not take effect immediately, for Congress, with admirable foresight, had provided that it would not become effective until a year after its ratification, which gave them ample time to stock their cellars before the great drought hit the country. By the time it became effective in January, 1920, Congressman Volstead's Act, which provided for its enforcement, had been passed. Unbelievable as it may seem, our nation through its legislative channels had, in effect, created a new commandment – "Thou shalt not imbibe." The country entered into what has often been described as the dry decade, a misnomer on two counts. Instead of a decade it lasted for almost fourteen years, and they were most decidedly not dry ones.

To prove that Congress had a benign eye for the farmers, the Volstead Act guaranteed them the right to make sweet cider, which of course turned into hard cider by natural fermentation, and the people of our rural area were not deprived of their usual beverage. Although they had not been in the habit of doing so in the past, the farmers resented the fact that they could not legally sell the hard stuff, and many became Scofflaws – a word coined to describe those who showed their contempt of the Act by flouting it. Some of them in our area doubled their production of cider in expectation of meeting the demand for it. Although they did sell some, no big demand for the product materialized as people wanted something with a higher alcoholic content. The sale of patent medicines, some of which contained fifty percent alcohol, boomed to such an extent that the federal agents began seizing them.

Demand for liquor and for places in which to consume it became bigger than ever. In the cities speakeasies appeared by the scores. As soon as the federal agents padlocked one joint two others sprang up to take its place, and they were heavily patronized. People who had previously avoided saloons found the speakeasies friendly and exhilarating. Women, who before prohibition would cross the street and go out of their way to avoid even passing the door of a saloon, began to appear in the speakeasies in ever increasing numbers. The Eighteenth Amendment emancipated women from the stigma associated with public consumption of liquor.

Nature and money abhor a vacuum, and strenuous efforts were made to supply the growing demand for liquor which was appearing throughout the country. One big source of supply was obtained by smuggling it over our border with Canada. Our farm was only about seventy miles from the border, and the road through our valley became one of the busy routes used by the rum runners. The speed chases and the maneuverings that took place between them and the federal agents who pursued them provided us with our major excitement of the prohibition years. Canada was happy to supply the liquor, and the thirsty population down country was happy to buy it, even after the bootleggers had cut it two or three times.

Rum runners and their rings were numerous, and they spent money freely. Many of the farmers along the route benefited by giving them quiet assistance. If a farmer's barn was close to the road, he would be paid to keep his barn doors open and his mouth shut. A rum runner who was being pursued could quickly disappear by driving into an open barn and closing the door. If it became necessary he could hide his load in the hay mow and reappear on the road with an easy mind. Even if the agents suspected the truth, they could not search the barn without a warrant, and by the time one could be obtained there would be nothing there but the cows. Some farms served as headquarters for the rum runners.

A Country Life

There were quite a few farmers who only farmed haphazardly, but they appeared to be prosperous.

At the start of prohibition many of the rum runners used Model T Fords. The federal agents had larger and faster cars, but the Fords were nimble. They could travel over roads which were too rough for the large cars to negotiate with any speed. A runner in a Model T traveling the Connecticut Valley could suddenly change his course by taking some old road which led over the hills to another watershed where he would have the choice of several routes. The agents did not have any communications with each other as they do today, and they were frustrated.

The one drawback to the Ford was that it could not carry a big load, and the runners began using larger cars. The one that became their favorite was the Hudson Super Six. It was a large car which could be souped up for speed and beefed up to carry a heavy load. It became the rum runners' work horse. The cat and mouse game of using old roads to elude the agents changed to an out and out speed chase that often took the form of a sportive game between the agents and the rum runners.

The rum runners were a wily bunch and were well organized. The cars which the agents captured were confiscated and sold at public auction where the runners promptly bid them off and put them back to work. A car loaded so heavily that it sagged to the axles would be vigorously pursued by federal agents, and it would lead them a merry chase over the countryside. When the agents caught up with it, they would find it loaded with bags of grain or some other innocent material. Meanwhile, a dozen cars or a couple of trucks with heavy loads of liquor would amble through town and along the route without any fear of pursuit. Country sheriffs and local police were only interested in their territory and were usually open to pay-offs.

Our small village was greatly surprised when one of its residents was caught driving a rum runner's truck. The truck and load were confiscated and he was fined. Sometime later the details of his employment became known. He had no idea who he was driving for. The only person he ever saw was the one who hired him, and he only saw him but once. All he saw were the trucks that he drove. He would receive a letter telling him when and where to pick up an empty truck that would be parked in some secluded spot. The letter would have explicit instructions as to where to park it in Canada and also when and where to pick up a loaded one. The switch between the two would occur either in Sherbrooke or Magog. There had to be some collusion between whoever he was driving for and the officers at the line, for until he was caught he never had any trouble getting his load across. He would park the loaded truck at some designated spot in the White River-Lebanon area and make his way home. In two or three days he would receive his pay for the trip in cash through the mail. When he was caught, a lawyer showed up and paid his fine, but his employment ended. He drove for several months and was sorry to lose the job, but he figured that getting caught ended his usefulness to the ring.

The White River area seemed to be a hot bed for liquor in the Upper Valley. It was an important railroad junction with trains from Canada going through daily. They probably played a part in keeping the area liquid. That was in the days of the Roaring Twenties: Joe College and the coonskin coat; rolled stockings and the fast stepping Flappers; bobbed hair and the hip flask. Dartmouth College must have played a large role in keeping the bootleggers in the area prosperous.

The rum runners of the coastal areas ran their cargo into bays and inlets by means of fast speedboats which were supplied by ships beyond the twelve mile limit. They were pursued by the Coast Guard who were no more effective in controlling them than the federal agents were in stopping the traffic through our area.

According to the reports of those days the liquor smuggled into the country by the rum runners furnished only a small portion of the market supply. The lion's share of the market was supplied by stills which were most prolific in the cities and which made the cheaper grades of alcohol. Some of them were large ones which could make one thousand or more gallons a day. There were innumerable small ones known as kitchen stills, designed to turn out a few gallons a day on a kitchen stove. Some of them made decent alcohol and others distilled rot gut out of garbage which could lead to blindness and paralysis in those who were unfortunate enough to drink it. It was not a nice era.

There were stills of all sizes in our area. One favorite ploy was for an operator to rent a farm and set up a large still in the silo. They were profitable. A man who used to run one told me that if he could operate a five hundred gallon a day still for a week it would be all gravy from then on, and that the loss of the still in a raid was not of much consequence as long as he could get away.

I never saw but one still at close range. A man from Canada rented an old farm house about three quarters of a mile up the road from us. I blundered into it one spring when I was woodchuck hunting. He had set up a still in the woodshed and had been operating for less than a week. We were both pretty edgy at first, but soon became well acquainted. I used to take him food two or three times a week, most of which came from the farm. We sold him milk, eggs, potatoes and some of my mother's bread. I thought that my mother would object, but she entered into the conspiracy and baked beans and pies for him. He told us that his name was Fred. He lasted a little over three months. I went up with some food one day and the place was abandoned. He had evidently anticipated a raid, for the still was buried in a hole in the yard which he had previously dug for the purpose, and we never saw or heard of him again. The still which he ran was a small one. I doubt if he made more than twenty-five or thirty gallons a day.

The general market was served by bootleggers. Every town of any size had several of them, and purchasing a bottle of spirits was a cloak and dagger procedure. Both you and the bootlegger were engaging in an illegal transaction, and he had to be especially careful. Most of them didn't care what they sold, and one had to take his chances as to what he was getting. The liquor which was run through our area was good Canadian Bond. Some of it was sold to the carriage trade, and it was expensive. That which was sold to the bootleggers was cut by them and diluted with caramel and cheap alcohol and other concoctions and sold as the real stuff. Bootleggers who could be depended upon to sell you pure uncut liquor were rare. An acquaintance with one of them was treasured.

One of my father's aunts married a man from New York City who was a tycoon. He was the head of a large store chain, and when the pressure upon him became rough he would come up to the farm for a week or so to relax. It took a lot of liquor to relax him, and it had to be the best. The only source that my father was sure of furnishing decent liquor was a farmer who lived near Plymouth, which was about thirty miles from us. He sold the liquor in half case lots which came wrapped in burlap. I accompanied my father on one occasion when he made a purchase. The farmer took few chances. After he had been paid for the liquor he told us where we would find it. It was cached under a large maple tree behind the roadside wall about a mile up the road. My father was uneasy with it in the car all of the way home.

Five Presidents coped with prohibition. Wilson was in office when the amendment became effective, but he was too sick to pay much attention to anything. Harding was far from being a teetotaler, and he more or less straddled the fence. Coolidge was well known for being tight lipped and had but little to offer. Hoover made a stab at praising it by calling it a noble experiment, which drew such guffaws that he kept silent thereafter. All of their administrations tried to enforce the Act, but it was like whistling to stop the wind. Roosevelt ran on a plank which called for repeal of the amendment and won by a landslide.

William S. Morse

He kept his word, and in February of 1933 the Twenty First Amendment which called for repeal was adopted by Congress. The states fell over themselves to ratify it, which was done in December of the same year.

After thirteen years and eleven months of depravity, a person could go into a store, openly buy a bottle of decent liquor and take it home without breaking the law.

Landmarks

It was around the middle of the 1940's when Paul Glover and I spent two days cruising Victory Bog and part of the headwaters of the Moose River, which is a wilderness area in northeastern Vermont. New England Power Company had a large acreage there at that time. They were contemplating building a storage dam, and were trying to peddle the stumpage off and get it cut before the area was flooded. They provided a local man who knew their land and the area to serve as our guide.

William S. Morse

We picked him up at Granby, left our car at the dam site, and started cruising. We followed our guide without paying too much attention to the course he was taking. Our main interest was in seeing the timber and in making sure that he didn't show us the same ground twice. Around the middle of the first afternoon we decided that we had better head out to the car and call it quits for the day.

After heading out and following our guide for some time without seeing any familiar ground, we began to sense that something was haywire and we started questioning him. He admitted that we did not seem to be where he thought we were, and that he was somewhat confused. His excuse was that we had spent the day in mostly low ground which was pretty well timbered and under a heavy canopy, and that he had not been able to get a decent glimpse of Old Umpire since we had left the car.

Umpire is the name of a mountain which is prominent in that area, and it was his landmark. We headed for higher ground where we climbed out of the timber until the mountain and the surrounding country came into view. Old Umpire enabled our guide to orient himself and we headed for home. We were a couple of mountains off course, and it was almost dark when we reached the car.

The same experience has happened to many people, and it illustrates the importance of landmarks and the necessity of keeping an eye on them.

● ● ●

A Country Life

We normally associate landmarks with prominent physical features of the land that are visible for some distance, but there are other types of landmarks. There are those which are a part of us and which are invisible. Many of those landmarks are inherent in us, and were bequeathed to us by our ancestors. Others we start picking up at our mother's knee, and as we progress through the years we are exposed to ones which are strange to us and we have to use great care in choosing which of those to accept. If our personal landmarks are not strong enough to have a lasting effect upon us, or if they are faulty, the results are not nice. If we lose track of those which we have, as we often do, we run the risk of becoming lost, or at least, badly confused.

According to legend, someone once asked Daniel Boone if he ever became lost while exploring the frontier wilderness west of the Cumberland Gap. He replied that he was never exactly lost, but that there was a period of a couple of weeks when he was God-awful bewildered. Eventually he must have found his landmarks, for he was instrumental in settling Kentucky and Missouri, and became one of the famous historic figures of our country.

There could be a moral in all of this. When we find the going rough and life becomes confused and bewildering, perhaps we need to head for higher ground in order to consult our landmarks and get on a better course.

First Edition

Capital City Press
Montpelier, Vt.

1995